GROWING

A STARTUP
IN THE DIGITAL AGE

Howard A. Tullman

Published in the United States of America
For bulk orders, please contact info@blogintobook.com

Perspiration Principles logo designed by James "Red" Schmitt
Special Thanks to Lakshmi Shenoy and Claudia Saric

To purchase all volumes of The Perspiration Principles, please visit:
BlogIntoBook.com/tullman/

ISBN: 978-1-61984-981-5

DEDICATION

Sitting down every week to write something that will be meaningful and ideally of lasting value to others is a lot like setting out to start a new business. Sometimes there's a germ of an idea; sometimes it's an emotional reaction or other driver; or perhaps it's just a problem or situation that needs to be addressed. And occasionally you simply want to see things change and no one else is stepping up to the plate to make that happen.

You can't know how hard, long or costly (in many ways) the journey will be and there are no guarantees that anything good will ever come of your efforts, but you know for certain that nothing will ever happen if you don't get the process started and try. It's a lonely path and every bit of encouragement, assistance and support that you find along the way makes the job a little easier and slightly more likely to succeed.

I hope that these books will be my modest contribution to your success and to the well-worn and tattered bag of hopes and dreams which we call entrepreneurship.

CONTENTS

Part II: Customer Acquisition & Retention

MAKE SURE YOU'RE GOOD TO GROW

In a recent fireside chat, Dennis Chookaszian, the long-time CEO of CNA Insurance and more recently a substantial angel and early-stage investor and advisor to numerous public and private companies, departed from the usual plethora of pompous pieties and platitudes that seem of late to comprise the primary content of far too many typical technology panel discussions and got down to sharing some concrete and very specific advice for startups, some concise rules of thumb and formulae which he uses to evaluate the likelihood of a startup's success, some thoughts about the criticality of scaling swiftly, and a few closing comments about the importance – early on – of paying attention to matters of ethics and the core values of the business you're trying to create. As I like to say, you can't build value if you have no values. See http://www.inc.com/howard-tullman/how-far-will-you-go-to-be-loved.html   In terms of sheer content, straight talk, and take-away value, this was one of the best talks and Q&A sessions we've ever had at 1871.

Dennis is a guy who – as much as it's ever possible to do so – has really refined his investment strategy and approach and made a science of how he looks at prospective investments. In addition, it was clear that he's thought long and hard about exactly how he advises young entrepreneurs on what they can realistically expect on their journeys and the best ways to prepare themselves and their companies for the very bump roads and precarious paths ahead. He noted that he's often approached by folks for help in raising early stage capital or providing senior level introductions for them to large firms and – as often as not – he says that while he could help, he won't - because he doesn't think that it's the right time for them to raise capital or that taking in investment capital (even if it's abundant and readily available) is the right approach for the development stage of their businesses. In the startup business, you eventually learn that a quick and honest rejection is a lot more helpful in the long run than a grudging or half-hearted favor that ultimately does neither party any good.

As you might expect, the discussion started with what he called the "rule of three" which is a simple way to think about the need to focus the scarce resources and bandwidth of the entrepreneur on the most critical and pressing issues for the business. He said that – as a general proposition – it's almost impossible to pay attention and devote your energies to more than 3 or maybe 4 critical concerns at a time. As Confucius probably should have said: "Man who chase too many rabbits end up with none."

The three most important areas that Dennis felt every startup needed to concentrate on were:

(1) <u>Substantial and Sustainable Revenue Grow</u>

If you can't determine early on who is going to pay you for your new product or service and you haven't demonstrated that the dogs are gonna eat the dogfood, then it's highly likely that you don't have a viable business. In addition, your business model and your actual results need to realistically demonstrate an achievable market size and a path to securing market share sufficient to show early exponential revenue growth. Dennis's shorthand for this criteria was T2D3 which meant that your year-over-year revenues were expected to triple in each of the first two years and then to double in each of the next 3 succeeding years of the business.

Dennis shared some very specific and detailed criteria with the group about how each business should look at the nature and quality of its revenues in order to determine whether they were on the right path. The four critical factors were: (a) businesses building recurring revenue bases are far better than ones dependent on constantly securing new business especially because renewals are much easier and less expensive to secure than new sales; (b) the customer retention rate of the business was absolutely critical – all customers are very costly to acquire and very easy to lose today in a world of almost infinite choices and alternatives; (c) businesses based on products or services having a steady stream of new customers or ones that required constant replacement or renewal (the "razor blade" model) were much more attractive than durable goods businesses (like selling refrigerators) where the products had very long repurchase or replacement life cycles and could even fairly quickly reach points of substantial saturation; and (d) businesses offering products or services which had a predictably high rate of obsolescence were much more attractive than those where the products had long useful lives.

Finally, Dennis was also brutally frank with the audience about how frequently startups fail. While he believes (as noted above) that the most recurring cause of early business failures is a lack of sufficient and rapidly-expanding revenues, he also noted the problem with pointless perseverance. He said that very often the biggest mistake an entrepreneur can make is trying to stay the course and waiting too long to bite the bullet and either pivot quickly or decide to shut the business down if it's not making the necessary progress. I like to say that there's nothing worse than profitless prosperity where your top line keeps growing, but there's no bottom line in sight. He pointed out that establishing some milestones or benchmarks for measuring your business's success over a fixed period of time and then sticking to those metrics either way – in good times or in bad times – in deciding your next steps is a form of management discipline that is essential. See http://www.inc.com/howard-tullman/the-future-of-tech-metrics-not-moonshots.html .

(2) <u>Resisting Raising Too Much Capital Too Soon</u>

Dennis is a bootstrapping hardliner. He doesn't agree with the "appetizer rule" to wit: that the time to eat the appetizers (or raise new money) is when they're being served or available. He believes that you should raise as little as you can for as long as you can regardless of how easy it might be at a given point in time to secure new funding. For a contrary view, see: http://www.inc.com/howard-tullman/tech-startups-take-the-money-and-build.html . He also said that you should only seek outside investment (and only as much of an investment as you realistically will need) once it's clear that you have an actual business with provable revenues that is going to grow and prosper. Otherwise the outside money will cost you too much and – probably worse for you and the business – conceal the fact (or defer the unhappy realization) that you haven't really figured how to operate and scale the business in a profitable manner. He noted that mega-incubators like 1871 are great places to get started because they enable entrepreneurs to avoid all kinds of costs and commitments that are bad uses of their scarce capital and – at the same time – to secure access to enormous amounts of "free" resources, education, networking and mentoring that will all be crucial to their long-term success.

(3) <u>Leadership and Ethical Values</u>

The smartest investors bet on the jockey and not the horse and nothing is more important for the success of the business than the strong leadership skills of the senior management team. And, because the required skills sets will change dramatically over time as the business grows, it is also critical that the management be sufficiently flexible that they can grow and adapt to the new requirements of the business.

Dennis noted that this is a <u>very</u> rare outcome and that it is unusual for the CEO of a startup to survive in that role beyond a certain point in terms of the company's revenue growth, market(s) size and share, etc. It's very clear that entrepreneurial and managerial skills are quite different and specifically the CEO's role and involvement in various functions and parts of the company will need to change materially as the years go by or the CEO will need to be changed.

What cannot change and what is critical from the outset are the values that the company develops and builds upon as it creates its own internal and external culture and, here again, it is the CEO whose behaviors and attitudes are the most critical in providing the essential role model for the rest of the company. Mission statements are a dime-a-dozen these days and all the talk doesn't mean a thing if your actions and behaviors aren't aligned with your professed beliefs and values. Over time, the values of each business will develop and the priority of certain concerns and considerations may change somewhat, but it's a very slippery slope that needs to be jealously guarded because it is very hard to ever recover from the damage that results from broken promises and commitments. By and large, values don't abruptly break; instead they crumble a bit at a time. I like to say that it's much, much harder to live up to 99% of your values than to honor them 100% of the time.

Dennis said that each of us needs to determine which values are most important and that we all need to establish an ethical framework. Once you have established those ground rules, it's crucial that you also make it clear that there are boundaries and bright, red lines which simply cannot be crossed. While people are people and we are all fallible, there are just some behaviors which no business can abide or afford. In other situations, some understanding and forgiveness and a second chance might be the most appropriate response.

In his view, everyone has a three tier ethical framework and the critical issues in each case are what behaviors are in each tier and then which tier a particular case of questionable behavior falls into. The three tiers are (1) Zero Tolerance; (2) Possible Rehabilitation; and (3) Everything Else. Behaviors which fall into the first tier are (1) honesty/integrity breaches and (2) any kind of abusive behavior. There is simply no way back from these kinds of problems and any proven violations must result in immediate termination. Violations that impair the core values of the business cannot ever be tolerated.

Other issues which fall into the second tier – personal problems, substance abuses or performance problems – can potentially be remedied by giving the offender a chance to correct the problem. But these cases must strictly a one-shot opportunity to get things straight and any repeated behavior needs to be swiftly dealt with and the person must then be terminated.

Everything else can and should be dealt with through the normal management and HR processes. By and large, these cases should not involve the senior management team. Only those instances which impact the business's basic culture and mission are serious enough, central enough, and important enough to be reinforced and reiterated through the involvement and behaviors of the business's leaders. People, since time began, have paid attention not to what we say, but to what we do. Some things never change.

PART I

SALES & MARKETING

YOU CAN'T SAVE YOUR
WAY TO SUCCESS

Every business owner understands that, in addition to the many internal factors which can make or break a business, the cyclical state of the economy itself can also have a material impact on the success of your company. To a certain extent, it's like the weather - we can bitch about it all we want and blame those no-good politicians, but - in the end - we have only a limited ability to change these external market conditions. However, that doesn't mean that anyone should be sitting around feeling sorry for themselves and waiting for their life to get better.

I love the old Chinese saying: "Man stand for long time with mouth open before roast duck fly in". Good things in business don't happen by themselves (except perhaps in the movies) and, if you aren't making things happen and moving forward, you'll always be losing ground. So, in my world, we don't whine about politics, circumstances or greener grass. We believe that the people who succeed in today's hyper-competitive marketplace are the ones who get up and look for the right "circumstances" and, if they can't find them, they make them. Everyone thinks about changing the world, but no one thinks about changing themselves or their business. But, as I've said before, if you don't do it, someone will come right along who'll be very happy to do it for you or to you.

We've been treading water for too long and FUD (fear, uncertainty and doubt) has made us way too conservative. The big guys have been cutting back on their R & D budgets for years to protect pennies of earnings and thereby killing any prospects for new ideas and real innovation. And the little guys (like us) have been saving our shekels and not advertising or promoting our businesses. We need to start investing aggressively in the future (like we really mean it) or many of us won't have a future to worry about.

Now's the time to push our products and services and to demonstrate to everyone that we have the courage of our convictions. Not when the whole world finally wakes up and jumps back into the fray. I like to think of this running ahead of the pack as "getting ready to get lucky".

And, when you press your bets and bet on yourself and your future, you actually accomplish three other important objectives:

(1) You effectively set the pace for the rest of the market and you can become the market leader even if you're a tiny company;

(2) You reassure not only your customers, but your employees and your vendors as well; and

(3) You can grow your business at the expense of your competition without spending a lot of money since they've pretty much left the playing field to you.

Keep in mind this simple fact: increased market share is taken and grown NOT in good times, but in difficult times when everyone else is sitting on the sidelines and nursing their wounds. In good times, people want to advertise. In bad times, they have to advertise. If you don't, you die. The minute you hit the brakes, you start to slide down the sales slope.

Here's a case in point concerning Saturn.

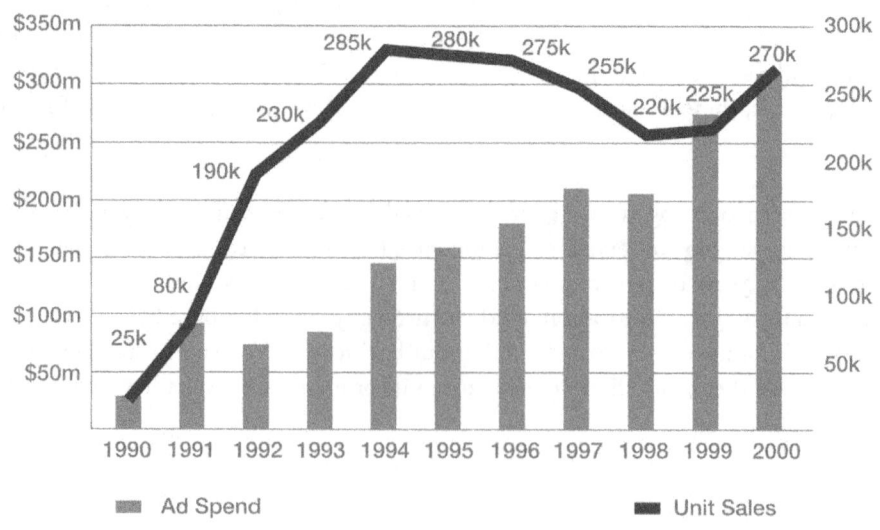

When sales dipped a tiny amount at the start of 1995, they started to cut their ad spending and that flattened 1995 and 1996 sales. Then they tried to get back into the game heading into 1997, but panicked when the sales didn't immediately recover and they cut back again on the ad spend. This killed not only 1997 results, but 1998 and 1999 sales as well even though they really accelerated their spend in mid-98. The bottom line (as the chart clearly shows) is that trying to "save your way to success" (or even to improved bottom line results) is like trying to catch a knife. Most of the time, you just can't do it and it's very painful even when you do.

And here's a little survey of 600 U.S. companies whose revenues increased after the 1981-82 recession and what they did with their advertising during the recession.

Companies <u>Increasing</u> Advertising – VOLUME UP 275%

Companies <u>Decreasing</u> Advertising – VOLUME UP 19%

It couldn't be much clearer. Ya gotta spend real money to make money. Doing business without advertising is like winking at a girl in the dark – you know what you're doing, but no one else does. And please don't try to do a bunch of things cheaply that you shouldn't do at all.

Bottom line: get going. There are a number of things – large and small - that every business should do <u>right now</u> (especially if you believe that there's even a glimmer of light at the end of this long dark tunnel) to prepare for the better days to come. But there's one thing that is absolutely critical to understand - in good times to be sure, but even more so in tough times - you can't save your way to success.

DATA IS THE OIL OF
THE DIGITAL AGE

I said two years ago that - by 2020 - 90% of the U.S. population would have willingly agreed to provide at least some of their personal data to the MAW. I'm starting to think that my estimate was too conservative. The global pace of massive data acquisition is picking up steam and speed and it's definitely an auto-catalytic process - the faster the changes come at us, the sooner the next changes start to appear. So you need to get moving just to hang on.

There are many explanations for the acceleration, but the main and most important change seems to be that no one expected that all of the diverse behavior drivers (inducements, incentives, trade-offs, etc.) would converge on each of us so quickly, specifically, simultaneously and, frankly, pretty much inescapably. But that's where we're at - stuck in the middle of the M.A.W.- and getting in deeper every day.

The M.A.W. - in case you're wondering - is my shorthand for today's replacement for that tired old whipping boy - the evil military-industrial complex - which we were all told - dictated and controlled our lives. The M.A.W. is slightly more benign so far in that it doesn't so much control our lives every day as it engulfs and overwhelms us 24/7 with emotional and economic sticks and carrots which continually impact and influence our behavior.

The M.A.W. (the omnipresent collision of (M)edia, (A)dvertising, and (W)ork in every part of our lives) is the real environment in which we're all now living. And honestly we've all become willing participants (to varying degrees) in the program and relatively happy campers with the deals we're making and the results because no one wants to be left out or left behind. Springsteen said "we're livin' in the future and none of this has happened yet", but he was wrong. It's happening right now.

And, by the way, this is another party to which I hope you're not waiting for an invitation. You and your team need to get into the data marketplace with both feet before your business get priced out of the game by greedy middlemen happy to resell the data to you at a premium (DSPs and others) and before you get shut out of the market entirely by faster and deeper-pocketed competitors who will absorb all the available inventory.

Keep in mind that the key notion above is that "we agreed" to share and surrender this information. God only knows how much of our own information we have inadvertently or unwittingly parted with at this point in time. I'm simply talking about the extent to which each of us has made a deal - a conscious transaction - where we have decided to trade and supply some of our personal data in exchange for some perceived value or benefit that we would be receiving in return. And by the way I don't mean "perceived value" in the pejorative sense as if these things weren't real and concrete. For sure, some incentives are virtual and slight at best (like digital badges and certain utterly inconsequential "achievements"), but many others have clear and direct financial and economic benefits.

What kinds of value or benefits are we talking about? The list grows daily. You trade your personal data because:

a. We're all basically lazy and would rather do less work than more – Do It for Me is a lot easier than DIY;

b. We hate wasting our time and re-entering the same info over and over in order to perform recurring activities of any kind;

c. We become "invested" in an activity as a result of our prior effort and commitment and we just tend (due to inertia) to keep going with the flow;

d. We've "connected" with others who are important to us in a shared context through the activity and it becomes convenient to continue and difficult to depart;

e. We develop habitual behaviors and habits (online or otherwise) are just really difficult to break or abandon without a reason;

f. We're actively "engaged" and "retained" by the smartest of the players so we stay; and/or

g. We receive direct financial rewards for our participation.

When you add these up, we're talking about saving you time, making you more efficient or productive, connecting you with a community or group that's valuable to you; or that old stand-by – making you or saving you money. In many of the cases, it does basically come down to money. Almost everything does.

One of the neatest new deals has been created by a couple of the largest auto insurers in the U.S. If you let Allstate (thru its *Drivewise* program) or Progressive (thru the *Snapshot* offering) track your driving activities for a relatively short period of time, you can earn major discounts on your car insurance. It's a "win-win" for anyone who's a decent driver. I call this "swapping surveillance for savings". And we can expect to see more and more offers and opportunities like this.

It's pretty easy with tools like *FitBit* and other biomedical tracking devices to think that many of our daily activities will soon be available for researchers, marketers, economists, behaviorists, etc. to pay us for and acquire in order to study and sell.

And, by the way, it's definitely a two-way street. You can also pay up to be left alone. If you're sick of being swamped with ads on your Kindle, you can pay up and cut them off. At the end of the day, it's all just math and money.

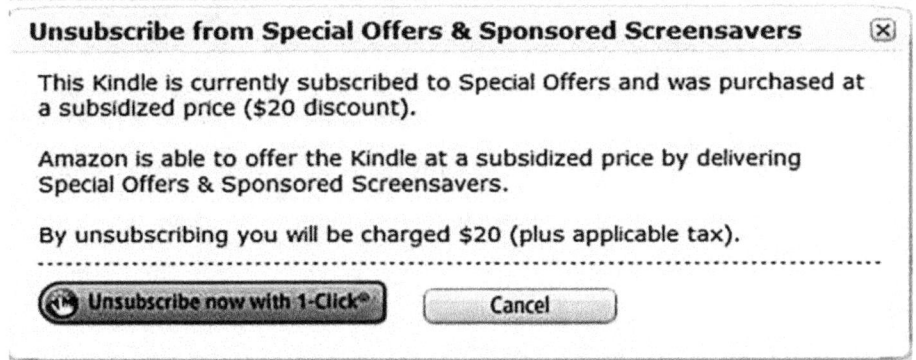

But here's the bottom line. We're all involved in competitive markets today and it's really an arms race which will be won by the guys with the biggest guns, the best technology, and, above all, the most accurate and complete data.

Think of this as fair warning – your competitors are grabbing the goods and dropping big dollars for data and, if you don't want to be left in the dust, you need to get into the game as well.

FORGET MADE-UP METRICS
& FALSE FACTS

Microsoft Excel is a curse. In its deceptive simplicity and ease of use, it has taught several generations of MBAs and entrepreneurs that creating the financial underpinnings for a serious business plan is basically just another form of word processing. It has insulated these aspiring business builders from the difficult and time-consuming - step-by-step - tasks of building a real case for a real business from the bottom up. Making a plan for the future without tying your analysis to the concrete experiences, results, and wisdom of the past is just a form of building castles in the sky.

As a result of the Excel explosion, we've seen the creation of thousands of mindless spreadsheets underlying hundreds of naïve business plans put forward by individuals who have relied on Excel to painlessly develop forecasts and predictions which haven't the slightest connection to any reality, but which look "marvelous" as Billy Crystal used to say. And then these folks (and their promoters, investors and enablers as well) seize upon these plans as if they were the Gospel expressed in rows, columns, and pivot tables and use them for support and borrowed credibility - rather than for analysis, guidance and hoped-for illumination – exactly the same way that a late night drunk relies on a lamppost. Welcome to the fantasy world of made-up metrics.

When you use a tool like Excel (that's fundamentally neutral) to generate hypothetical and hysterical numbers to make a theoretical case with no real foundation in fact or history and then you fall in love with the finished product, you're deeply into made-up metrics. Credible plans need to proceed from a serious grounding in prior, documented experience and results – they can extend those results into the future – I would call these "projections" and, while they are never certain, at least they are logical and well thought out. We used to call this process "precision guesswork", but at least we had a process and we knew where our numbers came from. "Predictions", on the other hand, are the results of those cases where people simply insert aggressive new growth numbers (without any clear justification, obvious cause, or decent explanation) and then use Excel to replicate, grow and run the numbers forward until they reach the sky.

When you get carried away with this approach, you tend to forget that building a real business is about producing results, not predicting results. It's actually easy to predict the future, it's just impossible to know when it will arrive. You can plan all the plans you wish, but you can't plan results – you have to do the hard work of making those happen – and that hard work starts with building a solid factual foundation for your numbers. Too many excellent Excel plans are just sterile exercises stuck somewhere between wishful thinking and delusion.

Another entire category of bogus business plans are crammed with so many fake facts and factoids and other accumulations of data that are only remotely relevant at best to the business being built. Grossed-up market size is always one of my favorites. "Our addressable market is everyone with two eyes in the world." Right. Fake facts are all the rage these days, but they don't help advance your cause. I think Seth Godin is a smart and thoughtful guy, but here's what he had to say in a recent blog post: "[Aside: More than a billion people on Earth have never purchased anything on sale at a store.]" Do you really think there's any factual basis for that statement? Why waste our time with this kind of stuff?

Even good facts are just facts – they're not props for arguments or support for conclusions – it's the conditions, trends, needs, and other market circumstances that you extract and extrapolate from the facts that help to explain, define and ultimately "sell" your business idea to investors, customers and partners. It's these larger drivers which you need to discover, document and master – and not cute anecdotes and fake facts – that will provide the real framework for the continual decisions you'll need to make as you move things forward.

Building a business in these tough times is about pushing your vision forward and adapting it where necessary through a sea of constantly changing facts and circumstances. But if you don't start with a fundamental idea – grounded in some reality – it's way too easy to get run around in circles or just lost in the shuffle. These are serious problems for young entrepreneurs because the triumph of the form of the materials over their real substance (slick spreadsheets) and misplaced reliance on irrelevant metrics (fake facts) can lead you to believe that you have your arms around your business when – in fact – you're swinging a big hammer, but you're trying to nail *Jello* to a tree.

WHEN THE ELEPHANTS DANCE, IT'S THE GRASS THAT TAKES A BEATING

I t's downright dangerous for small companies (and especially start-ups) to deal with the corporate giants who dominate so many industries. They're the pachyderms; we're the plant life. And like elephants, they have great memories and recall how the world was; but no imaginations to see the world that will be. Still, because of the size of their markets; the fact that so many of them are dinosaurs who don't see the deluge about to drown them; and the fact that timely innovations and new technologies will ultimately turn their businesses around or put them in the ground, these are the places where the people who want to be real players need to be.

Entrepreneurs with great ideas and enormous energy (but limited time, resources and access) face a number of specific challenges in circumstances like these, but there are 5 things to keep in mind which can dramatically improve your odds of success.

1. Right Church - Wrong Pew

It's easy to get lost or misdirected when you're wandering through the wastelands of these large companies. Too often people with new ideas get sent to (not to say "dumped on") the new media, innovation or digital guys and quickly forgotten. Typically the people who populate these departments are long on enthusiasm and short on cash and the ability to green light anything. It's critical to remember that big firms have many different pockets of serious money. If you spin your story correctly, you can often tap into community programs, marketing initiatives, charitable commitments or even diversity requirements – all of which are well-funded. Don't be shy about asking – sometimes success is simply putting a new cover on the same old book - or adding a novel twist to an old tale. But make sure before you start that you're in the right place.

2.   Right Pew - Wrong Seat

Even if you're in the right place with the right story, your proposal still needs to "fit" the customer's current interest and appetite. You need to make sure that what you're offering matters. This means that – when all is said and done – and you've busted your butt and hit it out of the park – and you've done it all with panache and a vengeance – you don't want to hear those two awful words from the client: "So what?" or something equally disappointing. You need to make sure that you understand the required size, scale and impact which will be needed to <u>matter</u> – to impress the client and his bosses – and to move the needle for them or you'll just have been wasting a lot of your time and energy. The problem is that even great results (high adoption percentages, significant engagement times, strong sharing and amplification, etc.) which are hugely significant and encouraging to the entrepreneur just don't matter if you're talking hundreds of active participants in your pilot and they're dealing with millions of card members or customers. I've seen major retailers do this over and over – they'll run almost any credible pilot project (especially one on your dime) for a new service or product, but they won't pull the trigger when the project is done because their metrics don't match yours.

And, if that wasn't bad enough, keep in mind that while start-ups run out of cash – big companies don't – and so they are more than happy to keep mediocre projects running for way too long – even though they may have mentally checked out some time ago.

3.   Right Seat - Wrong Guy

Another recurring risk in dealing with big businesses is that the guy sitting across from you can't say "yes". There are hundreds of people in these places who can say "no" – some of whom seem to have no other job than that – but you've got to get in front of the ones who can say "yes" and write the necessary check to put their money where their mouth is. As I have said before, you don't want to be dealing with the monkey when the organ grinder is in the room.

You've also got to be sure that you carefully explain how your proposal is incremental and additive to whatever it is that they are now doing and that it's not simply going to cannibalize their current sales or replace existing sales with less lucrative or valuable ones. We used to call these "kissing your sister" deals because they don't lead anywhere you'd want to be and you have a lot of motion and activity but no real progress or results.

4.　Right Guy – Wrong Time

I'm always amazed at how many entrepreneurs don't do their homework and understand the budget and buying cycles of their target customers and how these things are set in concrete and so tightly locked down that these people couldn't help you if their lives depended on it. I think this is because there really are no comparable restraints or barriers in the life of a start-up – everything is urgent, everything can be and needs to be done right now, and there's always no time like the present to do what needs to be done. But bad timing can be the quickest deal killer of all and – more to the point – if you show up at the wrong time, it's pretty obvious to the customer that you don't know much about their business, their calendars or their requirements. Don't make this amateur mistake.

There is one exception to this rule and that depends almost entirely on whether or not you have been lucky enough to develop a real connection and relationship with your buyer. If you have, then on occasion you will tumble into the *Alice in Wonderland* scenario where the buyer lets you know that – instead of their budgeted funds being totally committed and/or spent - they have excess funds which they need to spend before their budget year runs out to avoid having their budget cut for the following year. All I can say about these situations is – take the money and run.

5.　Right Time – Wrong Pitch

Sometimes the best way to get the order is not to try selling at all, but simply to focus on "helping" the customer understand the competitive dynamics of their marketplace. Fear is rampant in even the biggest companies and the greatest fear for many decision-makers is FOMO. The Fear Of Missing Out. Many market resources and opportunities are scarce or finite and letting these big guys know that there are other major players in the space who are about to shut them out is a very substantial and effective motivator.

One of my favorite old examples involves what I call cross-industry blocking alliances. These are cases where major players in different vertical market team up in a competitive game of musical chairs and the last company to find a chair (actually a partner) loses out big time and potentially for years thereafter. One of the great marketers of all times – American Express – was an early victim of this strategy and it cost the company millions of cardholders and billions of dollars. The story is very simple.

In the early days of frequent flyer programs, a very smart guy at American Airlines determined that miles could be used as an incentive not simply for flying, but for many other things (like car rentals and credit card purchases) as well. American quickly and quietly partnered with MasterCard. United in a flash (almost) partnered with VISA. And guess where that left American Express. Out in the cold without an airline partner which was credible and widely-available for business travelers. I suppose they could have partnered with Midway Airlines or with Greyhound and covered the bus market, but basically they were screwed for years. In the next several years, while AMEX topped out at about 9 million cardholders, VISA blew right by them and grew to almost 30 million cardholders in the same timeframe.

MAKE SOMETHING THAT MATTERS

I like to be supportive of almost any implementations of new, exciting technologies – even when I think that some are definitely "solutions in search of a problem" or the latest and greatest examples of "software that only the designer's mother could love", but there are limits and sometimes you see something so sad; so ill-conceived; and so poorly executed that you have to speak out just to avoid all of us toiling in these fields from being tarred and feathered with the same brush or beaten over the head with the stupid stick.

I'm very excited about the prospects of augmented reality across many different fields including education, entertainment, marketing, etc., but the recent *Haagen-Dazs* lid top "Concerto Timer" AR demo – available free in the Apple iTunes store [https://itunes.apple.com/us/app/haagen-dazs-concerto-timer/id670015815?mt=8] is so awful that it's likely to set the entire AR field back a century or two.

The premise is that you take the ice cream container out of the freezer and then you use your phone to download an app and then stand somewhere nearby and watch an AR-generated music video that appears on top of the ice cream container lid for the two minutes that *Haagen-Dazs* thinks you should wait for the ice cream to reach the ideal temperature for consumption.

The only thing that's remotely smart about the whole thing is the hook to a charitable donation for honey bee research and preservation for each of the first 15,000 downloads, but frankly, I'd pay the 5 bucks directly to the charity myself just to have the time back that I wasted on the demo and a promise that I'd never have to try to watch the thing again.

Where should I start?

(1) Who exactly is the audience and how old are they likely to be?

If anyone is experimenting with new, cool AR apps, it's tech-savvy kids and young adults – not grown-ups.

(2) Who thinks that kids today are listening to classical Bach violin pieces?

Bach Inventions No. 14 for violin and cello? Really? Have these guys spent too much time in the freezer?

(3) Who waits 2 minutes for anything today – especially ice cream?

We live in an IG world – Instant Gratification. Waiting for your wine to breath might make sense after you unscrew the lid. My ice cream melts in my mouth.

(4) Who is going to stand anywhere for 2 minutes (like an idiot) holding your phone precisely focused on a pint of ice cream while it "tempers"?

I thought it was painful to watch paint dry. But this is much worse and you only have to watch paint dry once. Here, because the video isn't persistent, it disappears the second you move your phone away from the lid so you have to stand like a mime (while your arm cramps up) to watch something you wouldn't choose to watch on a bet.

(5) Who can even see the image clearly or hear the music being played?

Using *Kinect* to capture the image of the performer rather than playing a clean, simple video (if you absolutely had to) was unnecessary and foolish overkill – like using a sledgehammer to kill a fly – and resulted in bad sound, poor video quality, and overall a completely disappointing experience. What were they thinking?

There are already plenty of intelligent uses of Augmented Reality technologies and some very smart applications that are finally getting traction and which even make good business sense because they supplement and add to the user experience instead of wasting our time. This clearly isn't one of them.

SHOW YOUR USERS
THE SHORTEST PATH

We have always been told (in a quotation wrongly attributed to Ralph Waldo Emerson) that, in terms of innovation, if we built a better mousetrap, the world would beat a path to our door. As it happens, the mousetrap (as we know it today) was invented a few years after Emerson died, but this hasn't prevented the issuance over the last hundred years of thousands of patents for new mousetrap designs along with additional thousands of failed mousetrap applications.

But what's the smartest strategy for a business when the guy or girl next door has already built a better mousetrap? Within reason and the bounds of legality, you'd think that the best plan would be to copy his or her solution and incorporate it into your own processes as soon as possible. Instead, over and over again, whether it's because of our own egos; some unstoppable craving for originality; the "not invented here" syndrome; or just expensive stupidity, we insist on re-inventing even the best wheels.

Now, I'm sure there are instances when pure ignorance is a reasonable defense – if you don't know there's a better way, it's hard to criticize you for not adopting it. I'm also certain that the vast majority of even the most conscientious website managers and marketing gurus don't know that there are new tools being brought to market every day which can help you quickly discover how your business is performing in a competitive context and how your website (or, as I used to call it, "your front door") stacks up against the competitor down the street or across the country. I'll tell you about one of the newest and coolest analytical tools (*Pathful*) in just a moment.

If you're not making it quick and easy for your site visitors and prospects to find quick answers, simple solutions, and a short path to success, you're making your life a lot tougher than it needs to be. And if you can readily determine that your competitors are doing a better job than you are in this area, then the solution is simple. Copy their best approaches and practices and make them your own. Frankly, this is nothing to be ashamed of – it's happened since the beginning of time. This is the reason that there used to be gas stations on 3 or 4 corners of the same intersections or why there are "car dealer" rows and auto parks where competitors sit right next to each other. A good location is a good location. The fact that the other guy may have gotten to that corner first doesn't mean squat unless you're too proud or foolish to park your business there as well.

So what does this mean in the simplest terms for your website? Well, *Pathful* is a new young Chicago-based company that's built some basic tools which can quickly and objectively tell you how effectively your website is doing its job. How well it works – how quickly it gets your customer to and through the point of purchase - because, as they say at *Google*, data beats opinions.

So this isn't a question of how pretty or cool the site is. There's no data point for "cool". And who really cares how much Bob likes it – even if Bob's the boss. His opinion is just that – an expression of one man's preferences and prejudices – not a way to set a smart strategy or build a great business. I'm all for educated guesses and your intuition is sometimes a big help in moving from a "so what?" solution to something spectacular. But start with the facts as your foundation. And that's what *Pathful* can help you do – answer the two most critical questions as to how you're doing and how you stack up against the competition in terms of the operational effectiveness of your site. Getting your customers to their goal so that they give up their gold.

Pathful's analysis addresses and answers a lot of questions and concerns, but the two that always jump out at me (and which are clearly interdependent) are the following: (1) Speed – how quickly can I get to the answers I need? – and (2) Clarity – how clear and free of distractions and detours is the path to success? Here's a simple case in point where 5 different organizations websites (A, B, C, D & E) were tested head-to-head on the Speed spectrum and graphed against Satisfaction. No surprise here – we don't like to wait – we want our answers and we want them now. And the longer we have to wait, the less positive our experience. And, if that wasn't bad enough, keep in mind that this analysis relates ONLY to the people who toughed it out and got to the finish line – not to the large numbers of people who bagged it at various points along the way because it just wasn't worth their time or continued effort or they ran out of patience.

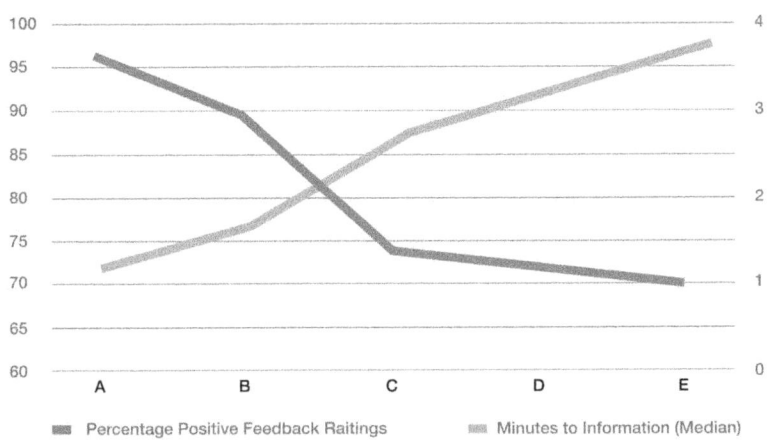

COMPARISON OF "SATISFACTION" TO TIME TO GOAL FOR 5 SITES

The second equally significant component was Clarity and the analysis there was equally instructive. I'm only going to show you the best path and the worst path of the 5 (the displays are a little unwieldy), but you'll get the point. The squares are the right steps and the circles are detours and distractions. These paths proceed from the top of the charts down and – even though each of these two sites had basically 4 steps to get to the finish line – you can clearly see how easy it was for people to lose their way on the worst site – and how often that happened.

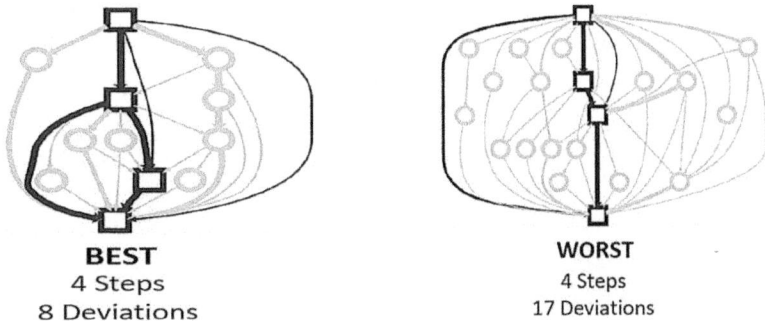

BEST
4 Steps
8 Deviations

WORST
4 Steps
17 Deviations

COMPARISON OF TWO SITES' PATHS TO GOAL

This really isn't rocket science. Think of these charts as potential roadmaps for your business, get in touch with *Pathful* or some other source of comparable and objective data, and get busy.

MAKE MORE MOATS

I'm always surprised how often even very sharp entrepreneurs don't understand the importance of always making sure (through repeated and consistent communication with their team) that, even as their people are chasing new sales opportunities and falling in love with the newest and coolest marketing tools and tricks, they aren't losing their focus on the basic blocking, tackling and execution that help to consistently pay the bills. Essentially this entails nothing more than taking really good care of your existing customers. This may seem a bit old school and even a little boring, but it's a tried and true way to build an increasingly valuable enterprise.

I have always called this basic business strategy "knocking on old doors" which means working harder to deepen your connection to and your involvement with your current customers and thereby to increase their average spend ("share of wallet") as well as to lock them in for the long haul. It's critical for new businesses to always remember that customer churn is the ultimate enemy of increased profitability. In the frenzy of a hot start-up, it may appear that customers are easy to come by because the adoption rate of anything shiny and new these days is remarkably high. But the abandonment rate is 10 times higher than that and if you're not quickly connecting with and retaining these new customers, they'll be gone and you'll be running on a treadmill and going nowhere fast.

Your existing customers (the newest and the oldest) are already in your system and you're already regularly interacting with them (hopefully effectively) so - rather than spending scarce money chasing new customers or trying to steal customers from the competition - you just need to do a better and more expansive job of servicing the guys you've already got and the cumulative results – particularly year over year - will knock your socks off.

It's pretty much a given that happy and "cared-for" customers will simply end up spending more with your company over time. And "organic" customers (basically home-grown) regularly spend LOTS more with better margins than customers acquired through one-off marketing spends, promotions, and other incentives that may attract incremental customers, but don't create lasting connections to them. Think of the pain and suffering caused to thousands of small restaurants by Groupon 1.0 which drew tons of "cheapies", but few returning "foodies".

Happy customers also boost your business and your profits in other ways. They not only buy more (and at better prices); they are also easier and less costly to service; and they're a great and active source of referrals. Especially in the new age of tech-enabled social media, constant connectivity and collaborative commerce, this is the "new" news.

An active, well-run program that drives, encourages and rewards ongoing and authentic customer recommendations and referrals (and incents them to take ownership of the relationship) will generate 5 to 10 times the bottom-line results in terms of actual revenues as any of the other traditional tools including trade shows, print media, and even direct, in-person sales calls. And the results are far more obvious and measurable as well.

You can pretty much forget entirely about trade shows – they're toast. Expensive, inefficient and unfocused: they burn out your people; generate a bunch of worthless leads from lookers, not decision makers; and divert your attention from the things that matter most. If the real decision-makers are even "in the house" at these things these days; you can be sure that they aren't walking the floor and looking for you.

Similarly, in most businesses today, the people still using printed media are so far behind the curve that they might just as well take the money they're spending on creating and delivering print solutions and burn it. In fact, I think – especially in older traditional markets like car sales – that more print/newspaper advertising is driven today by inertia and superstition than by smarts or strategy. You hear older dealers (usually in businesses not run by professional managers) say: "It's how we've always done it – why should we stop now?" Scary, but true.

And frankly, even ignoring the growing presence, utility and efficiency of net-based meetings and demos and video conferencing services, the math today for most products and services simply no longer makes sense or justifies having your sales people on the road trying to sell new customers face-to-face. Wining and dining might be great for your sales people, but from the perspective of busy management personnel in well-run businesses, it went out with the 3 martini lunch quite a long time ago. Good managers want decision-making data about proposed solutions presented as quickly and clearly as possible and they want it now – not in two weeks when the salesman can stop by.

And, if you asked them, your existing customers would also tell you that they're perfectly happy with regular phone updates and new product suggestions or even timely email communications if they are properly managed and valuable rather than just random and unfocused promotional materials. This is known as "the ATM phenomenon". Is there anyone left in the world who would rather deal with a bored and borderline teller rather than a rapid-fire ATM machine for virtually any banking transaction? By and large, if you take a careful look, you'll find that your customers feel pretty much the same about their interactions with you and your sales force. Especially if you have a strong CRM program in place which is primarily focused on capturing the lifetime value of each customer.

But strong, long-term customer connections don't happen by themselves. You need to continually and aggressively work on new ways to keep your customers engaged and invested in the success of your business (as well, of course, as in the success of their own businesses). This process is pretty well understood, although rarely consistently executed.

But the less well-known and clearly under-appreciated tool for customer retention that's even more important because of its competitive deterrence as well as its retention benefits is the need to do everything in your power to increase your customers' switching costs. This is what I call the process of "making moats" which not only keeps your customers in the stable, but also makes it much harder for the competition to reach them and induce them to move. Effective "moats" can come in many forms, sizes and shapes and only you will be able to quickly determine which are the easiest and most cost-effective for you and which make the most sense for your customers.

Keep in mind that I'm not talking here about things like long-term contracts with overlapping expiration dates or similar "legal" constraints which keep folks in the fold. I'm talking about arrangements, value-added tools and data, and other barriers to switching or leaving which arise as a result of things you build and deliver in the ordinary course of your business operations which actually improve the customers' experience and also – as an added benefit – make it much harder for some other competitor or vendor to steal them away.

As I said, the examples are too numerous to list, but there are three industry characteristics which will help you discover and develop the moats which will matter the most in your business.

(1) <u>Complexity</u>

The more that you can do to streamline and simplify essential, but complicated processes for your customers and increase their productivity by saving them time and avoiding redundancy; the "stickier" your connection with them will become. Sometimes these may be complexities built into your own systems, but more likely these are aspects of doing business within a given industry or system where you can accumulate and share – exclusively with your customers – procedures, documents, regulations, and other resources that are necessary to the business, but not necessarily readily-accessible or even known to occasional users. Pre-populated forms; access to associated information like applicable state taxes; drop-down lists and boxes with regularly used choices and selections; embedded estimators and calculators, etc. are all valuable add-ons and the more detailed and industry/user-specific your incorporated add-ons (think of these as "power tools") can be made; the more valuable they will become to your customers and the harder they will be for competitors to replicate.

(2) <u>Compliance</u>

Many industries are more highly regulated than most people can imagine and it takes years of painful and costly experience (often through trial and error) to develop the internal resources and personnel who are sufficiently skilled at navigating these regulatory environments to permit a given company to successfully compete with other established players. But, in many cases, these companies come to rely very heavily on their vendor/partners because a substantial amount of the industry wisdom and compliance knowledge is actually in the hands of the vendors rather than the companies themselves. This is primarily because the vendors are regularly interacting with the state and federal regulators on behalf of multiple clients and parties whereas a typical company's involvement will be much more infrequent and sporadic. The more that you (as a vendor/partner) can add additional functionality and the products of your broader experience to your offerings (turning your "products" into more valuable "services" and consulting), the more locked-in, the customers become.

(3) <u>Consistency</u>

As strange as it may seem from the outside, in many cases, it is often the third-party vendor/partners of large corporations who are the ONLY parties who actually have the data and the ability to advise and assure these large, unintegrated organizations that their various departments, divisions and affiliates are operating in a consistent fashion across the business and in a manner consistent with the company's own rules, regulations and policies. To a certain extent, this is another value-added service where you have the opportunity to provide quasi-managerial functions for your clients who simply don't have the internal capacity or organization (or sometimes the necessary information systems) sufficient to handle these tasks themselves. They really can't tell the left hand what the right hand is doing and they operate at their peril (especially in highly-regulated industries) because of this. As a result and as you begin to gather and archive more and more information about their business's functions and organization, you become an increasingly unique and valuable asset and basically irreplaceable. In an era with increasing management and employee turnover and diminishing institutional memory at all levels, being the keeper of the company's operational history and one of the few places they can turn to assure compliance and consistency throughout their company is a powerful lever for your business and a major deterrent to your competition.

Bottom line: if you want to hang on to your customers for the long run (which is really the name of the game for successful businesses) and go beyond the basic CRM programs that are table stakes these days; you need to erect exit barriers (moats) which raise your customers' switching costs; provide substantial disincentives to migration; and help to exclude competitors. Focusing on their needs to reduce complexity, increase compliance and assure consistency throughout their businesses is the key to keeping them.

DON'T WEAR OUT YOUR WELCOME

Having been in sales for most of my adult life (and frankly what entrepreneur isn't always "selling" something), I try to never be rude to even the most clueless or incompetent salesman because I know what a tough and thankless job sales can be. But recently I stopped taking one guy's calls and began just hanging up when he started directly calling my cell phone. (I've also been ducking my barber's calls, but that's a different story.)

All I can say is that I'm very grateful for Caller I.D. these days because – although most of the time I'm strong enough not to hate, this guy was treading on the thinnest of ice. And why? Because he simply wore out his welcome and – with me at least – once you've burned that particular bridge, there's really no way back. Life's just too short to deal with ignoranuses. And, in case that's a new word for you – it's people who are both ignorant and assholes.

But the saddest part of the story is that I went out of my way to give him all kinds of fair warnings. You can't push a rope no matter how hard you try and I fundamentally wasn't interested in what he was selling at the time. Unfortunately, he was just in too much of a hurry to hear me – even assuming (which might be a stretch) that he was interested. The truth is that it's a very thin line between persistence and pestilence, but it's pretty bright and obvious if you're paying attention and listening to what your prospect or customer is saying. This shouldn't be that hard a concept to master.

The fact is that all long-term success in selling always comes from two things – even in this crazy, time-constrained and chronically impatient world in which we are living – building relationships and being patient. And, by the way, I can't believe that I'm saying this – the world's most impatient guy and a long time sufferer of hurry sickness, but it's actually true. Trying to press a sale on an unwilling buyer at the wrong time is a waste of effort and energy. Patience always achieves more in the long run than force and, as I always say, even the strongest "No" is just a "No" for now. But not if you burn down the place and wreck your relationship in the process.

In sales, you're always dealing with people's perceptions which can shift in an instant – they're erratic and discontinuous – so, for a long time, you're it and the next moment, you're out - if you're not careful to thread the needle between obnoxious and irresistible.

I've got a few ideas and suggestions to share with you to help you think about ways to keep the conversation moving forward without crossing the customer's comfort line and throwing out the baby with the bathwater.

(1) <u>Small Serial Successes</u>

Great sales people will tell you that winning is almost never about hitting home runs or bowling someone over in a first meeting with your bravado and BS. It's about solid and consistent base hits – an unbroken series of successful gestures and increments - that lead over time to a relationship based on trust and then a sale. There are times when it's more important to walk away and wait for the real deal than it is to grab a quick sale (whatever your sales manager might think) which may or may not make ultimate sense for the customer. You have to learn to communicate a sense of urgency without seeming to be in a hurry. If you can't move things forward, it's a good time to move on and wait for a better moment.

(2) <u>Someone is Always Selling</u>

As they always say about stocks, they're not bought, they're sold. Selling is about momentum and – at any moment in a conversation – someone is selling – it just might not be you. If you find yourself leaning back on your heels and suddenly on the defensive, you've lost control of the conversation and, most likely, you've just met a master salesman who happens to be your prospective customer at the moment. You always want to be selling from strength and not seeking sympathy or someone's pity. It's OK to agree with your customers and even to empathize with them and all of their problems – as long as you don't end up (with the tables turned) agreeing with their very good reasons for not buying your product or service. And one more thought on this topic – as soon as you start talking about price – you're on the slippery slope and headed in the wrong direction. It's better at that point to pick up your marbles and pack your bags and come back when you're got a better story to sell.

(3) Sell Something Else

When you're selling something that nobody really needs, you'd better actually be selling something else. This is why perfumes are sold by smell, sex and status rather than dollars and cents. And why alarm systems are sold by images of burglars and broken glass – by smoke, security and safety concerns – and almost never on price.

(4) Manufacture "Maybes" and Reasons to Return

In sales, closure is as bad as cancer. A million "maybes" are better than having the door definitely shut in your face. So it's important to always have a plan to prolong the conversation; to have something (however modest) that the customer can say "Yes" to; and to always have a reason to return. Good selling is telling – explaining without a hidden agenda – adding to the customer's knowledge base – and being an impartial source of this type of "education" – and even of juicy industry gossip – is a way to make sure you're welcome to return.

ONE IS THE LOVELIEST NUMBER

Effective competition has always been multi-dimensional. One-trick ponies and businesses that were strong in a single area (product, technology, sales or marketing, etc.) but short in others rarely succeeded in the long run. By and large, there wasn't enough time to fix their shortcomings before the fast followers not only caught up, but quickly provided solutions which were quicker, cheaper, easier to implement or just better designed and more responsive to the real needs of the market.

The first movers and pioneers often identified and defined the problem, developed early approaches and simple solutions, and made all the early mistakes that are always part of the process and they basically set the table. And then, in too many cases to even count, an army of imitators rolled right over them and ate their lunch. One rule will never change – in the end, consumers don't ever care who was first, they only care whose product, service or solution is best when they're buying.

And today, I think it's an even tougher game because some of the fundamental terms of successful competition – especially for start-ups – have changed and the winners (as always) will be the companies that catch on quickly and respond to the new conditions. Sometimes that means moving forward and sometimes that means getting back to basics. These days, we're in a world where there's plenty of capital, there're more than enough customers, and there's even a growing talent pool in many industries and areas.

The competition today is not for capital or resources – it's for the consumer's attention and – for better or worse – you're competing for that attention – not simply with your direct and indirect competitors – you're competing with EVERYTHING that gets in the way of or in front of your message. Don't believe me? Check out your phone (which we do on average 150 times a day) and just scan your messages and news feeds. Family, friends, photos, phonies, ads, alerts, offers – it's unending and filters aren't much help so far. In fact, the initial GOOGLE filters are worse than no help – they actually make more work while you try to find buried messages and important information that some machine or moron at GOOGLE decided weren't worth your time.

It's just a fact of life that the channels to the consumer (and to all of us as well) are congested, confused, clogged, and increasingly costly and it's just way too easy for your message to get lost or drowned in the deluge. Media today is everything that gets in the way of communication. And there's only one thing that could make the situation worse. Spending money that you don't have and can't afford to waste on pushing out a confused or muddled message.

So we're back to that very basic idea that - in communicating with your customers and prospects - getting your message right is even more important than getting your message through. And here's the deal – one is the number. One message, one voice, one spokesman – end of story.

If you're the entrepreneur, I'm hereby giving you permission to tell everyone else to suck on it. It's your show, it's your story, and it's your game to win or lose. And – in the end – it's not about a rampant outbreak of the Egola virus (and don't let anyone else tell you otherwise), it's about effectiveness.

(5) It's Never Everybody's Turn

I realize that a company consists of many people and that many of them are making important contributions to the growth and development of the business. But I just don't care about them or their hurt feelings when they don't get their turn on TV or in the spotlight. Find other ways to recognize and reward their contributions. Democracy isn't a virtue in effective messaging – consistency, image, clarity and communication are all that matter. Let the whiners be the co-captains of the company bowling team.

(6) It's Not Really About You

It's always possible that you aren't the best spokesman for your business or that you're not comfortable in the role. If that's the case, just find the best person you can for the job. I'm assuming that you're smart enough to know your own limitations and desires. (Of course, if you can't successfully sell yourself and your idea, you might just as well forget about being an entrepreneur anyway – although I do realize that the selling doesn't necessarily have to be done on TV or in the spotlight.)

The real point is that – if you do sign up to do this job – it's not an ego thing – it's because it's hard enough to get a clear and concise message out there into the world and the more you can simplify the process - streamline the ideas and the images – and structure the conversations, the more successful you will be. You could teach other people over time to do this, but it's a waste of time in the early stages of the business to even try. Just do it yourself – it's faster and far more impactful.

And keep in mind that delegating your messaging to anyone else – especially outsiders and consultants – is a total disaster. The media may not know much – but they do know the real thing when they see it. And messengers and middle-men just don't work anymore. Like it or not, entrepreneurs today are mini-rock stars and that's who they folks want to see and hear from.

(7) It Really Does Work – Especially for MSM

The media doesn't know anything other than what you tell them. They're lazy and time-constrained. The easier and faster you can make it for them – think one-stop shopping – the happier and more responsive they will be and the more often they will be back. They need "go-to" guys and girls – experts and advocates - not inarticulate amateurs or losers who can't clip on a lav. They don't want a dissertation or a skull session – they want a sound bite. And they're just as grateful to get your message – quickly and easily – as you are to share it with them. Remember that it's not about education – it's about entertainment and selling suds and soup. You're just filler between the ads so they don't all run together. So make your message your ad – short, sweet and smooth.

And that's the drill. Just do it – over and over again – every opportunity you have – obsessively and repetitively. Repeated messages are remembered messages. Stay on message – people take a long time to listen. Don't apologize – don't share the spotlight – don't play nicely with others. Just get out there and get the job done. Even the wanna-be web stars in your company will eventually thank you.

EVERYTHING IS BETTER BY THE BYTE

For better or for worse, in today's autocatalytic technology-driven world, where every change accelerates the speed and frequency of the changes to follow, gamers (of all ages) are the virtual canaries in the coal mine. The disruptive innovations and the market transformations which the gamers' behaviors consistently predict are felt and rapidly found across every industry sector and, in general, across the board. As gamers go, eventually (and increasingly quickly), so goes the rest of the world.

It was the gamers' rapid abandonment of expensive, bulky and static gaming consoles (Playstation and Xbox) in favor of light, portable, and mobile devices which not only built companies like Zynga into almost overnight market leaders, but, much more significantly, presaged the world's online migration from the desktop to the mobile world. Mobile today is everything and everywhere and our smartphones are the direct descendants of yesterday's handheld gaming devices.

And there's still much more to be learned from the actions and choices being made by gamers every day which will change the ways in which more and more businesses price their products and services and the manner in which they interact with their prospects and customers. We're looking at the end of fixed pricing for anything and entering an ala carte/all the time world. Bulk packaging, bundled products, and even bargain pricing are all breaking down in favor of a single consumer demand driven by a desire for freedom of choice and flexibility – I want "everything by the bite" – whatever I want, whenever I want it, and wherever I am. And it's the gamers who have shown us exactly how these demands will soon find their way into every business.

It's helpful to start by looking at which approaches didn't work over time in the gaming space and why they didn't.

First and foremost, subscriptions and long-term commitments haven't achieved anywhere near the scale and player penetrations that were anticipated. The fundamental reasons are fairly clear – commitments of any kind and continuing obligations are out. Any online game company will tell you that the most active participants won't commit to spend a dollar in advance, but will spend ten dollars – a dime at a time – all day long.

Second, fixed pricing, downloadable paid games and pay-per-play models have also failed. The only companies making real money today (over a million dollars a day in virtual sales) are the companies deploying freemium games where players are charged for upgrades, increased weaponry, powers or skills, or other virtual goods.

So what are the lessons for the rest of us? Three basic propositions underlie the gamers' decision-making process and these ideas are already on their way to your market and your products and services if they're not already there.

First is Investment

The best and smartest games let the users set the effective price of each session or game each time they play. Some days it's a little bit and some days it's a bundle. The point is that the customer is in control. Your pricing strategy needs to incorporate and evidence the same kind of flexibility.

Second is Commitment

The best and smartest games let the users decide how much or little they want to spend each time they play. Some days it's a lot of time or money (each being a material kind of a commitment) and some days it's just a lark to kill some time. If you do things right, you can be all things to all people all of the time. But your products and services need to be accessible across a broad spectrum of pricing and consumer choices and not a simple set of fixed offerings.

Third is Valuation

The best and smartest games let the users decide on exactly how much the experience is worth to them each time they choose to play or continue to play. All the market research and pricing guidance in the world doesn't compare to just letting the customer determine the value of the experience. If your products or services provide real benefit and value to the users, you will discover over time (and over the lifetime of a continued customer relationship) that your best customers will actually pay up for the right experiences rather than try to be bargain basement buyers.

And focusing on the value of the experience is doubly significant because today no one under the age of 30 really cares about possession or frankly about owning anything. Everything is about utility and experience. Social and sharing. Ownership (buying "stuff") is a burden today – not simply because so much of the readily-disposable technology we see and use every day is outmoded and obsolete in roughly the time it takes us to master the things in the first place – but because, in addition, we would just as soon not assume the obligations and the commitments that come as part of the package.

Bottom line – I know that one size, one model, one strategy will never work for everyone – but one thing is true beyond question and that is that your best buyers will tell you that everything is better by the bite.

SMART REACH – BE THERE WHEN THEY'RE BUYING

I've been talking for several years now about how important it is to appreciate that – in today's complicated, ADD-addled, and increasingly cluttered and noisy world – it's become mission-critical in trying to sell anyone anything that marketers understand the new imperative that how, when and where you reach your prospects (and your existing customers) is at least as important as the content of the message you are attempting to deliver.

It's absolutely clear today that the <u>context</u> in which your message is transmitted and received by the target is MORE important to its successful communication and reception than the construction, creativity and even the contents of the message. I call this idea "Smart Reach". Smart Reach is all about the need to deliver engaging, demonstrably relevant, content to your target at exactly the right time(s) and place(s).

And here's an initial hint – in the game today, it's not just about "different strokes for different folks"; it's about fashioning radically and consistently different messages to be directed at the same folks depending entirely on the times and places and contexts in which you're attempting to reach them. And it's also about understanding and appreciating that to do this right; you need an entirely new formula: you should be spending no more than 25-30% of your time and energy of creating new content. The rest of your resources should be focused on planning, channel selection, distribution strategies and real-time measurements of the results so that you can course correct and better shape your campaign as it rolls out.

It doesn't really matter these days whether your content (or offers, incentives, etc.) is the coolest unless it reaches the right audiences. And, because content (standing alone) isn't laser-sighted or heat-seeking; it's gonna need serious help. Just like the fat old chicken sitting on top of the fence post, it's not gonna get there all by itself and it's not gonna get the job done without planning, positioning and an aggressive and focused push from you to help break through the channel clutter and reach the customer.

A staggering number of folks who you'd think were otherwise fairly intelligent don't seem to realize that their <u>literal</u> competitors (the sales folks and businesses who are out there selling directly competitive offerings and competing every day for market share in the same sectors and industries) are only a relatively small part of the problem. You don't get to compete for the sale until you win the race and the constant competition for the consumer's attention.

And in competing for the customer's attention today, which - right along with our time in general - is the scarcest resource we have, the list of distractors, obstructions, barriers and filters just continues to grow larger and longer every day. You're up against family, friends, breaking news, sports, music, medical issues, travel, charities, every kind of media, and even sleep-deprivation. And believe it's hard to sell new shoes to someone taking a snooze or a noon-time nap.

And that's why no one can afford to get these things "almost" right. Today, as always, "almost" only counts in horseshoes and love – not in the marketplace. And almost everything is easier to get into than to get out of – so it's critical to get off on the right foot with the right focus. There's too much money involved, the stakes are far too high, and the consequences if you misfire or waste your ammunition with poorly-timed or poorly-placed salvos are dire. They don't beat you – they just send you home and give the prize to someone else. And I recognize that there's no simple solution or crystal ball to tell you in every case or in any case what the exact right approach should be and that will be a determination that you'll have to make on the fly and over and over again. I certainly don't know and the thing that's for sure is that one size or one approach will never fit every case.

But let me give you just a new idea and a couple of questions to think about as you're analyzing your own programs which I hope will give you a new perspective on the problem. It's a very simple and time-tested idea. You want to be there when the customer wants to buy what you're selling. Because that's the only time that matters and it's a short window that opens and shuts in a snap.

But because you can't really read their minds (yet), you need to settle for the next best thing – smart reach. Think about (a) <u>where</u> you want to engage your targets and (b) <u>what</u> they will be doing when you do and (c) <u>why</u> that's the best possible time for you to make your pitch to them and then figure out how to get your message in front of them – at that time, in that place, and in the context of what they're doing. Reach me at the right time and I'm all yours. Reach me at the wrong time; interfere with or interrupt something that I'm doing which I regard as more important at the moment; get in the way of my friends or family or even my work and you've just wasted my precious time and your scarce and now wasted money.

Context is king.

IF YOU WANT TO BEAT BABE RUTH, DON'T PLAY BASEBALL

I wrote recently about "smart reach" and the need to understand that how, when and where you reach your prospects (and your existing customers) is as important as the content of the messages you are hoping to deliver. People who are socializing aren't likely to be in shopping mode; people who are chatting aren't generally consuming; and people digitally scrapbooking aren't really looking for new medications – whether they may need them or not.

These days the context (where they are and what they're doing) often trumps the content (what you're saying or selling) <u>unless</u> your messages get both active engagement from the consumer and are accurately aligned in terms of your target's time, interest and attention. Blindly launching your campaigns into indiscriminate channels (regardless of their aggregate volumes) like *Facebook* where the active users' likely behaviors aren't coincident with the actions you seeking from them is just too sloppy and too costly an approach for virtually any business today. These channels are readily accessible; they may even relatively easy to use and to measure (at least in terms of tonnage but not real reach); and they may not actually appear to cost that much (ignoring the obvious opportunity costs). But there's very little economic benefit in wasting your scarce bullets on bad marketing regardless of the CPMs or per-piece cost. And, frankly, these days the crowd in general is crap. You need to focus on the folks who matter – not the masses – and make your message real for them.

These mega-channels are simply the wrong places to be looking for new business or anything else unless you have thoughtfully crafted and precisely targeted your messages. It's exactly like spending the night looking for your lost keys under the nearest street lamp. Not because that's where you think you lost them, but because the light is so much better there. Lazy marketers use these big fat channels because everyone else is doing the same thing. It's like a drunk uses that same street lamp – for support (and comfort) rather than illumination.

To succeed today, you need real visibility into relevant behaviors and a strategy/ plan to move yourself away from the crowd and to do your own thing. If you want to beat the Babe (or the big guys in any business), change the game. That's why, while understanding context is certainly an important consideration to keep in mind and one that you need to take into account when developing your marketing plans, it's only one dimension of the new data and metrics-driven approaches to digital marketing that are changing the game and increasingly distancing the winners from the also-rans.

To really understand what's going on (especially in terms of the ongoing social conversations which, for better or for worse, are impacting your business every day (whether you realize it or not), you need to focus on (a) the <u>multiple</u> dimensions of these social conversations; and (b) who's having them; and (c) who's listening to them in order to spend your time, energy and resources wisely and, more importantly, to be sure that you are targeting and successfully reaching the right audiences.

Today, the fact is that no one with a brain wants to reach millions of easily influenced nobodies – regardless of how many fractured flicks they watch every day or even how many "allegedly" fervent (and generally faithless) followers they may have. Even faithful followers only matter to a marketer if the reason they're following an influencer is directly connected to the messages they're trying to extend and expand. Asking a Justin Bieber fan about Bach is a lot like asking Mrs. Lincoln how she enjoyed the play.

The only goal that really matters today is to get your messages in front of highly influential people (think digital multipliers and megaphones) who are tightly connected to significant (and fairly sizeable) niches of active and desirable individuals whose actions and attitudes they can directly influence (amplification) and whose behaviors as consumers, voters, or other cohort members you are looking to change and direct into actual results – not wishful thinking.

To do this successfully, you need to look at the whole story and at <u>all</u> <u>four</u> of its sides. Even more to the point, the big guys in the social listening spaces (*Radian 6*, *Buzz Metrics*, etc.) are all myopically focused on just one part of the equation (**WHAT** is being said and the apparent sentiment associated with it) and – as a result – if you hurry, you can jump ahead of them and deliver some valuable and truly-differentiated products and services to a marketplace that is ready, willing and able to buy anything that makes economic sense and that makes common sense out of the tsunami of meaningless data that they're swimming in right now.

As noted above, equally as critical to effective social listening and deliberate message delivery is a determination of **WHERE** the conversations are taking place (context) and information about **WHEN** the conversations are taking place (time). But it's the 4th dimension – the **WHO** is speaking and what are his or her relationships and connections to the ultimate target audiences as well as his or her ability to amplify and extend the messaging thru expressions that sway and influence (power to direct or drive behavior) the targets that is the vast unmined terrain and opportunity zone.

Klout.com and *Kred.com* are the pioneers in the individual influence measuring space, but at best these are mechanical attempts to count frequency, volume and potentially the extent of one's connectivity without a great deal of time or thought being devoted to the true weight, value and influence of the sum of these connections. These are brute force approximations and solutions that are barely workable and of little real value beyond generating some industry bragging rights and hype. This, of course, didn't keep *Lithium Technologies* from buying *Klout* recently for $200 million. I wish them lots of luck in figuring out exactly what they got and what to do with it.

But bigger and better versions of these types of tools are desperately needed because the stakes are high and so – as a result – are the opportunities for new disruptive entrants into this space. It's clear that today even the best language parsing engines and related algorithms are no match for the old family connectivity trees built out of bright colored Post-its tacked to the wall or the white boards that we see every night on the tube in the police procedural shows like *Law and Order*. You can't tell the players without a program and a scorecard and the best computers can still only do our bidding (and massive data assembly), but not our thinking (yet). The companies which build the products and services that help us identify, reach and influence the people who matter (the highly influential and deeply connected prime movers) and who – in turn – can move the markets and the marketplace will be the next generation of big winners.

We don't care about the wisdom of the crowd; we only care about the wisdom of the people we care about.

HOW DO I GET MY APP
ON YOUR PHONE?

I sit through lots of meetings these days wondering how so many smart people can be so oblivious to some of the web's harshest realities. They work so hard and they're so creative in most parts of their business and yet they consistently overlook the singly most obvious shortcoming in their plans for global domination. These aren't mediocre mopes or deluded dreamers – they're great technologists, really sharp systems engineers, dynamite designers and even prominent professors. But, far too often, as they pitch their products, services and amazing ideas, what always comes through to me is the sad fact that they just don't get it.

What's the horrendous hiccup? Ya gotta get it out there before it's gonna do you any good. I call it Digital DARE which stands for Distribution, Adoption, Retention and Engagement. If you can't get your mobile application on my phone (distribution) and convince me to initially try it (adoption) and to then keep it on my phone (retention) and finally to use it on a recurring and fairly frequent basis (engagement), you've got nothing to talk about. And each of these steps in the success path presents different challenges and hurdles.

I see this same syndrome with all the new frenzy around content marketing. There's a fierce focus on content creation coupled with "Field of Dreams" fantasies about the ease of digital distribution. The hard truth is that if you're not spending almost as much time thinking about (a) how your message will reach its intended targets (and how you will know [measure] that it has) as you are on (b) developing the message itself, you're just kidding yourself.

In the old days, when we were still talking about desktop computers (before the world moved to mobile), we used to say that "if it ain't on the screen; it don't mean a thing". The point back then was that ideas and talk were cheap whereas execution and delivery were much more difficult. Fascinating features and functions didn't cut it if they weren't in the code base. And all the wonder and wishful thinking in the world wasn't going to get the product shipped and launched. Then, once you shipped your product, the bar was quickly raised again and, at that point, distribution and penetration were the whole ballgame. Yes, that was way back then, but it's just as true and as critical to your success today.

And while the screens we're dealing with may be smaller and much more mobile, the job is still exactly the same. Distribution and adoption are all that matters in the first instance and the competition is tougher than it has ever been because, while there are billions of phones in the aggregate out there in the world, each and every individual user gets to choose what occupies the prime positions on his or her own device. It's just like the real estate business – location and placement are everything. As I've said now for several years - the scarcest piece of real estate in the world is the front screen of the smartphone.

And if you think the adoption curve on cool new technologies is quick; wait until you see how fast these fickle fanatics abandon the latest and greatest anything in favor of the next bright shiny thing coming down the road. Especially anything that's a novelty rather than a necessity. Not only is nothing the future forever; the fact is that it's hard to hang on to a prime position even from week to week without some powerful staying power. The basic rule is: "out of sight, out of mind". Getting there is plenty hard; staying there is harder still. If you're depending on me looking for it; you better be sure that I love it or I'm not gonna make the effort.

So, if you want to be taken seriously (however amazing your application may be), you've got to address the critical concerns which will be front and center in every investor's mind. And while there are no simple solutions, it helps to spend some time thinking about the different ways that you can get over the hurdles and who can help you in the process. Because especially today, these things take tough teams and strategic partners. They never happen by themselves because no one has the time, talent or money to bring it home all alone.

Think along these three dimensions:

(1) Utility - Make It Multi-Purpose

The more functionality that your application provides; the more value it creates for the end user and the more likely it is to succeed. In addition, engagement and retention are frequency games – the more reasons I have to use something; the more instances in which it saves me time or money; the more likely I will be to retain it and keep it close at hand. But don't make it bulky. Feature creep and too many functions is a sure formula for failure. Interestingly enough, excess complexity is exactly why *Facebook* is now slicing and dicing the FB mother lode into a series of single purpose mini-apps. But it's a doomed effort because the sheer number of the individual mini-apps will assure the eventual abandonment of many of them simply because the vast majority of consistent users (MAUs) will pick a couple of core favorites and forget the rest. I realize that it's a straddle, but the winners will be the ones who strike the right balance.

(2) Ubiquity - Make It Multi-Channel

The more channels and locations through which the end users can encounter and obtain your application; the more likely it is to find its way onto their devices. This is all about distribution partnerships and about engineering as many different "win-win" formulations with channel partners as you can manage to put in place. You want to be everywhere the user looks and the "go to" solution for whatever problem or need you're addressing. If you do this right, you're going to spread your application's availability horizontally across the universe of uses in multiple channels and this will provide you another significant advantage against individual vertical channel solution providers who simply won't be able to match the volume and scale that a single multi-channel horizontal solution can achieve.

(3) Universality - Make It Multi-Cultural

You've got to go global from the get-go. Sure the U.S. is a huge market, but it has never been easier or less expensive to make sure that your solution is available and works around the world. I hear stories every day about the power of the web and especially the cloud and how users – acting entirely on their own - are adopting new products or services world-wide without their makers spending any material marketing dollars or trying to put a bunch of feet on the street. Make it easy to go big and broad. Just like the most successful global movies are short on explication and long on explosions; you want your application to be a vehicle that basically doesn't care or even know about the identity, language or other attributes of the content processed through it. This is precisely why photos work so well in so many contexts and sharing applications. What you see is exactly what you get – no more, no less, and no one cares.

YOU DON'T GET A SECOND CHANCE TO MAKE A FIRST IMPRESSION

I call this the *Head & Shoulders* rule: most of the times in business you don't get a second chance to make a first impression and yet that simple fact of life is by no means as obvious and well-understood a phenomenon as it should be. Since we're talking here about "real life" and there are no second acts, rehearsals or do-overs; it's critical to make sure that the first impression people have of you and your business is at least favorable - and ideally - fabulous.

We're designed by nature to make lightning fast decisions (it's all an outgrowth of our earliest "fight or flee" instincts which were developed for self-preservation and to keep the animals we encountered from eating us) and we make these kinds of snap judgments hundreds of times a day without even thinking twice about them or the process. It's a visceral operation – mainly subconscious - and it's far more accurate (in 99% of the cases) than many people and especially behavioral "experts" like to admit. Turns out you can judge a book by its cover. Just not in the ways we used to think about these things.

In the old days, if you wore crappy old clothes to go out and look for a new car (which might or might not have happened to have been clean), the car salesmen would size you up in a flash and basically either ignore you completely or hand you over to the newest and youngest guy on the floor. Today, if you wear those same old duds to go car shopping, after, of course, you've checked everything out first on the Internet, the salesmen can't take the chance that you might be a major "in the money" code monkey or a mobile mega-millionaire and so they have to try to treat everyone who walks into the dealership in the same fashion.

But while this approach might be good rules of the road for the car sales biz and you can get away with dressing like a slob while you're shopping; it's a different story in any social or business context where the decisions you make in terms of your dress, your appearance, or any other aspect of how you elect to present yourself to the world) can influence – for better or worse – other people's impressions of you, your values and your ability to make smart and appropriate choices. People don't know how smart you are when they first meet you; but they can tell in a flash – based in some cases on nothing more than your appearance – that you've made some woefully bad choices sometime in the past. And it's a very short hop from there to "I don't care" or worse.

So we're still judging books and people by their covers – we're just drawing different kinds of conclusions from the data – less about economic circumstances or purchasing power and more about attitude, competence and overall good judgment. This is not to say that you're not always free to ignore other people's impressions and reactions and make your own choices; it's just to remind you that these are, in fact, conscious or unconscious choices that you're making and that all the choices we make come with consequences. And as you get older, you learn that who you are and what kind of life you get to live is largely the sum of all the choices – good or bad – that you've made along the way.

I recently wrote about one part of this problem in connection with the question of what to wear when you go on stage for your Demo Day pitch. See http://www.inc.com/howard-tullman/does-your-demo-rock-how-to-fix-that.html. I thought that your team's t-shirt was probably the safest bet of all, but mainly I was trying to suggest that you stay within the basic guidelines and avoid overdoing it in any direction – you don't want the way you're dressed to become a distraction. And the last thing you want to happen as you walk on to the stage is to have anyone looking <u>at</u> you rather than listening <u>to</u> you.

Crazy clothes, hiked-up heels, and bushy beards all subtract substance, attention and focus from your story. I realize that there are plenty of smart and savvy people who choose to dress or wear their hair in a certain style, but in this narrow context, I think that a fashion *faux pas* can start you off with a crowd that wonders if you're serious. Why would you want to start with that extra monkey on your back? This is a steep enough slope as it is – starting out in a rut of your own making – makes no sense. You should "make your statement" some other time and place.

And there's another monkey that it also makes sense to avoid if you can. Good people (that is to say most consumers) are somewhat patient, largely understanding, and – most importantly – inclined to give almost anyone the benefit of the doubt. But when you present yourself in a fashion that feels more like desperation than design or style; and you put it out there with an "I dare you to say something" attitude; you forfeit the benefit of the doubt.

Now the stakes are changed and you've got to do everything you're doing <u>really</u> well because you've essentially given up the standard margin for error. If you're gonna be right up in my face; you better not slip up because it's a very slippery slope and a very long road back. Make the slightest mistake and the person standing opposite you changes in an instant from "Get Along John" to "Judgmental Joe". People go from neutral to negative in these situations in seconds. We've all been there and done this ourselves.

So if you're gonna have tats all over your body or nose rings in your nostrils; just understand that you're walking a tightrope of your own making. On any given day, you can make it across with no problems, but you've made the job a lot harder and more perilous than it needs to be. And don't think that it's easy to fix the situation or repair the damage with a smile and a few sweet words. You can't talk your way out of problems that you behave yourself into.

WHAT'S REALLY WRONG
WITH RETAIL?

Where should I start?

Best Buy is bombing out. They should think about changing the name to Better Buy as in "better buy somewhere else that's gonna be around for the next few years" just in case you need them. It's morphed into a bunch of mini-showrooms for the mobile phone and computer companies and a hands-on demo facility for Amazon shoppers who want to handle the goods before they order online. The increasingly random product mix and the way they change their in-store locations so often make it almost impossible to find anything. It's like a torture maze designed by Conan the Floor Planner. Basically, they're spread a mile wide and an inch deep trying to be all things to all people and to have a little bit of everything for everyone and it's an impossible mission.

The concept of the long tail works – but only in the virtual world - for a simple reason. The web permits <u>infinite inventory</u> which no one in the real world has the cash, the resources or the shelf space to replicate in terms of its breadth or depth of available alternatives and choices. This is one of the main things that killed Blockbuster. Back in the day, we used to call them "Boxbuster" because they stacked tons of empty VHS boxes all over the store to make you think that they actually had something in stock that you wanted to rent (like a hot new hit film) once you asked for it. But when you did ask, nada.

Sears/Kmart (remember Sears?) is also sinking like a stone and they just cut Lands' End adrift for no greater or more apparent reason than they gave when they bought it in the first place. It was a desperate attempt to move upmarket and it went nowhere. Saying doesn't make anything so – you've actually got to change your actions in order to change your culture and to change the public's perception of your position in the market. This stuff doesn't happen overnight even if you're actually committed to making it happen which is somewhat of an open question in Sears's case. Similar attempts to reinvigorate and modernize their sub-brands like Kenmore and Craftsman have also been stillborn. Sears is a proud and historic brand, but it's probably just history these days. Some things are beyond redemption or salvation. Shopping at Sears is a chore and today no one's looking for more work.

And Radio Shack – the original store for geeks, model makers and operators of all sizes and shapes - is a wreck in the midst of the greatest boom in demand for technology and gadgets in history. If anyone had a chance to naturally migrate their business from hobbyists and Trash 80s to the big time in computing devices, it was these guys and they basically got rolled over by everyone else. In addition, with the whole world moving from analog to digital, they completely missed the movement from physical "kits" to digital everything. The Maker movement was their last best shot and they never even stepped up to the plate on that one. At this point, someone just needs to tell these guys to lie down because they are badly burnt toast.

Sears is in no better shape than Radio Shack. Nothing's worked since the Kmart deal. Kmart buying Sears was like taking poison to get even with your enemies and expecting them to die. It's another case of identity loss. Walmart (480B) owns the low price position. You could make an argument that Target (73B) owns the middle-class style and fashion spot although probably not for long – way too many new players moving into that space – and there is no more fickle class of consumers than their targets. And Sears plus Kmart (36B) owns nothing. They have no direction, no passion and no soul. Everything they do these days is short-sighted – it's like wetting your pants in a dark suit. It gives you a warm feeling for a little while, but no one else notices.

How did it happen? First and foremost, they all got caught to varying degrees in the muddle in the middle. Or maybe in the middle of the muddle. Today to compete effectively you just can't be beige or average and their stores and their offerings were basically "so what" in every possible category. If you don't stand for something in the consumer's mind and carve out a demonstrable and defensible niche, you're nothing. You can't save yourself with advertising, promotions, coupons and circulars – these days any kind of "brute force" spray and pray advertising (regardless of the channel) is just the unavoidable cost of being boring. And the proof of the pudding is that there are still companies getting it right. Interestingly enough, they are also still way too reliant on the old-fashioned techniques, but their in-store chops are second to none.

Maybe the best example today is Costco which has clearly figured a bunch of this stuff out. And considering that they started 20 years after Walmart which is the 800 pound retail gorilla, it's impressive that they are doing more sales today (109B) than

Target and Sears combined. What exactly do they know that the others don't and why is it important to your business as well?

(1) Family Fun

They've made it fun for the whole family (even Dads) to go shopping again. They've made it an adventure (instead of a chore) to hit the store and see what's new. They get that we're deep into the Entertainment Economy where every environment needs to be immersive, informative and engaging. And they have figured out that the main reason that all the stats suggest that the lion's share of typical consumption decisions are controlled by Moms is because the Dads aren't there most of the time when the shopping takes place. Once you add Dad back into the equation, the average spends of trips where two parents are present (rather than just Mom) increases by more than 40%.

(2) Here Today, Gone Tomorrow

The guys who run Costco are also masters of FOMO – Fear of Missing Out. Every other big box store tells you that they have unlimited quantities of everything to convince you that they will never run out of what you're looking for. Costco convinces you every week that it's your very last chance to grab that item or you'll never see it again. Why else would you buy your Xmas decorations in the middle of October? It's because you sincerely believe that, if you don't, you'll be totally screwed, your family will gleefully remind you of what you missed out on for months thereafter, and you'll be the only one on your block who didn't grab the goods while the gettin' was good.

(3) Run and Gun

They also understand that we all live in a world where IG (Instant Gratification) is the name of the game. I want what I want and I want it now. And they don't leave these things to chance or to even the smartest computers. They know that, while you're waiting in the checkout line, you've got next to nothing to do and that's when their super-salesmen descend with their scanning guns to check out the contents of your cart and let you know how much you will be saving – right then and there – if you switch up to a higher level of membership. In fact, if your order is big enough, you might even come close to covering the annual bump in the membership cost while you're just standing there and – for sure – if you're a regular volume shopper, you'll be miles ahead of the game in just a few weeks. It's easy, it's true, and it's right there – right now.

The moral of the story is pretty clear and simple. The expectations of consumers and customers are progressive – to hold their attention and their affection, you've got to keep making every new visit an adventure and an experience. If you don't, they won't be your customers for long.

CARING AND SHARING

A long time ago a very wise old man said: no one cares how much you know until they know how much you care. The ability to consistently demonstrate this type of paramount "personal" and emotional concern to others (about whatever the current issue or matter under discussion may be) is an essential ingredient in the make-up of any successful politician (or husband). We absolutely prefer sweet, "sincere" and somewhat stupid leaders (like Uncle Joe) to serene and severe smarty pants (like President O) who we know in our hearts don't care a fig for us common folk and, basically, would just as soon not dirty their hands dealing with our pedestrian problems. You just can't let those minor day-to-day disappointments get in the way of your grandiose thoughts and big dreams. And if you don't ever deliver on the dreams, well who's really counting anyway – let's just move right along to the next fundraiser.

And, when we (as consumers, customers or an entire country) feel like this, we proceed to act accordingly - by withholding our approval, our support and, most importantly, our commitment. President Obama's functional failings (too many to count) and basic inexperience and incompetence are nothing compared to his complete inability to manage the drama, emotion and theatre of the Presidency in a way that not only instills some (admittedly fast fading) modicum of confidence in his operating abilities, but - much more materially - convinces us that his Spock-ish heart is occasionally in the right place and in our corner. Where's that master of empathy - Doc "Bones" from the Enterprise - anyway when we desperately need him in the dawning age of Ebola?

We don't hear too much these days about anyone being the smartest guy in the room anymore (as if he ever was when either Clinton was within the same zip code), but we do believe that our President's trapped in a womb of his own making surrounded by the same unskilled and useless advisors that he's had around him from Day One plus some guy whose main job is apparently to keep the basketballs inflated at all times. Forget the nuclear football that we used to worry about having close at hand at all times; now it's all about tee times and clean, white Titleists.

You might regard this all as both old news and cheap politics, but managing these types of emotionally-charged interactions and exchanges (where – as often as not – the customers don't tell you the real problem or their actual feelings until: (1) it's too late; (2) the connection with them is irreparably broken; and (3) they're long gone - is also a critical component of how you and your business need to carefully approach the new world of "social" everything where everything's a two-way conversation and everyone gets a vote whether we like it or not.

Today, the context is somewhat different, but the fundamental idea of demonstrating your interest and concern to your intended targets hasn't changed much. The basic objective is to figure out how to make me care and then how to make me share. I'm happy to spread and even amplify your message (as long as it relates to and resonates with me and is delivered at the right time, place and context) by sharing it with my friends and throughout my network as long as I actually believe that the message, the concern, and the process are all authentic. So how do you go about getting it right? And who exactly knows what they're talking about since the majority of the people talking about this stuff have: (a) been doing it for about all of 5 minutes and (b) couldn't find their asses with both hands even if you gave them a hint and a head start.

Sadly, right now, there are about a million people full of suggestions, systems, tools, tips and tricks of the trade for making this whole social thing happen for you – social media consultants are definitely part of a growth industry where there don't appear to be any required credentials although being the biggest blowhard on your block is a definite benefit and being a diva in your own mind doesn't hurt at all either. It also helps to be in your early 20s just as it does in Hollywood where a bunch of equally ill-equipped and uninformed folks are running businesses while they keep looking over their shoulders hoping that no one will figure out that they have no idea what they're doing either.

And then there's also a growing number of morons and scam artists who think that you can "fake it 'til you make it" in this social media business. I'd say they're having roughly the same degree of success as the guys who thought that the makers of Preparation H should also make a lip balm while they were at it. I wrote about these bozos a while ago in these pages. (*The Trouble with Social Media*. http://www.inc.com/howard-tullman/the-trouble-with-social-media.html). Sadly things have only gotten worse with pseudo experts on "virality" being all the rage today. There's a reason that the blind leading the blind don't end up getting anywhere.

I'm not sure that anyone has all the answers for your business (or that the best answers won't change again by next week), but there are three basic ideas that it's important to keep in mind as you develop your own social media plans.

(1) Less Messaging is More Effective (A Little Goes a Long Way)

Just because you can doesn't mean that you should do certain things. High on that list is inundating your intended targets with tons of repetitive email, interruptive and inconsequential texts, run-of-the-mill offers, mixed and confusing messages, etc. – all of which are doubly destructive. First, by burying your important communications in a pile of non-stop crap, you lose any prospect of commanding the attention of your targets and you also run the risk that your channel may be shut down entirely either by the end-user or by the email guardians in the sky. As the poets used to say, if I had more time, I would have been briefer. Second, by bundling the important material with the mundane and mediocre mass, you cheapen the entire set of messages and make it easier to dismiss your whole effort. There's a reason that people hate bulk mail and it's not just its weight and crappy production values. If you're respectful of my time and interests (and at least semi-polite while you're at it), I'll be happy to help you get the word out.

(2) Give Me Ammo, not Ads (I'll Be Fine)

Information-sharing is a contact sport and it's also a highly competitive one. People – especially those who regard themselves as major influencers in any area – don't just want to know what's going on, they want to be the first to know. But they're not looking for the run-of-the-mill chatter that *Access Hollywood* or *Tech Week* had last week, they want the straight goods and they want the good stuff that will position them as knowledgeable and in the thick of things. Factoids and fluff aren't going to move anyone's needle – you need to develop real facts and substantive information that will stick and stand up to scrutiny and then you need to get it out to your advocates and net promoters as soon as possible - before it all becomes yesterday's news. The bulk of active social sharing now takes place in a matter of hours – the same day - not some days thereafter – and if you miss the first wave, your message will just get lost in the froth that follows.

(3) You Can't Push a Rope (You Won't Have to)

Save your breath and save your money. If you have the right message and a great story, you don't have to sell anyone on selling it for you. The people you want to reach (for their influence and their ability to build your story) – the major influencers in any space - are like the scorpion who rode across the river on the croc's back and then stung him anyway. When the croc asked why (after the scorpion had insisted that he would never do any such thing), the scorpion replied – "it's my nature – it's what I do." Here's the dirty little secret – you don't have to chase or push these folks – just like the scorpion, they also can't help themselves. They have to share and they have to push these stories out there or they fear that they'll no longer be relevant themselves. So don't sweat the distribution part of the program until you've built a rock-solid and valuable story and then let it fly. Sometimes the best push you can provide is to take a step back and watch things happen from the sidelines. Never let 'em see you sweat.

LEVERAGING LATERAL LEARNING

I wrote a few months ago about the importance of keeping your eyes open for opportunities to grow and expand your business outside of your core markets and expertise by looking into "adjacent" areas which would afford you the chance to extend your product and service offerings into new geographies and across other dimensions and vectors without substantial new investments or even significant changes in the basic elements of your programs. See http://www.inc.com/howard-tullman/five-reasons-your-market-is-bigger-than-you-think.html.

I called this basic concept "sliding to the side" which meant attacking readily-accessible and proximate markets along new lines which might include identifying and targeting who the new customers were, what the required and desired offerings might be, and/or where, when and how your products and services were going to be delivered in order to meet the needs of the customers and clients in these new markets. This was an idea based on looking outside of your traditional market and sector definitions and then moving in directions that might well be outside of your comfort zone, but which offered rich rewards if you were successful and only modest financial penalties (and probably some wasted time) if things didn't ultimately work out. That was an *inside/out* approach to growing your business.

Equally valuable and again - something that's right before your eyes (if you're looking) - is the idea of lateral learning which is an *outside/in* approach to improving how you are doing things. Basically, instead of working to extend your areas of impact and influence beyond the virtual four walls of your business, here the new idea is that you explore, examine, evaluate and incorporate the best approaches and ideas you can find outside of your own shop and you pull them all into your operations as quickly and seamlessly as possible. You're never going to have all the great ideas yourself or develop all the best solutions internally, so feel free to copy or steal the best of breed answers from anyone and any place you can. Just don't copy their mistakes. Keep in mind that while education is something that is allegedly done to you; learning is something you're responsible for doing for yourself.

I call this concept "lateral learning" and here's the secret: you will absolutely learn as much or more from the people working around you (both in your company and outside) about how to step up your game and improve your prospects as you will from any mentor, teacher, class, book or lecture. When it works well, you discover that you're looking at things you've always thought you've known and understood, but in new and exciting ways. Think of this process as stepped-up and hyper-intelligent osmosis – where you consciously increase the focus and the energy devoted to checking out what and how others are doing things – some even better in the moment than you are – so that you can ultimately get to the point where you look around and no one's kicking your butt or doing your business better than you. Get started today and see what happens. There's no limit to what you can learn if you're not afraid to ask or too embarrassed or shy to inquire. But learning doesn't happen by itself – it's got to be part of an ongoing program and commitment to continually iterating and raising the bar.

And the fact is that you can try this strategy any place and in a variety of ways. But there is no better place to take advantage of learning laterally (from your peers, neighbors, role models and even competitors) than installing yourself in an active and constantly growing startup incubator (like our best-of-breed 1871 facility in Chicago) where there are literally hundreds of businesses in a single massive space and thousands of people working every day to create, develop and grow them every day. When most people talk about why young entrepreneurs should try to get into an incubator (or accelerator), they often focus on some of the obvious emotional components ("it's lonely trying to do this stuff on your own"; "there's a lot of energy and encouragement available in these places; etc.), but it's the serendipitous learning and the amazing synergies and happy accidents that happen every day in these environments that are the things that will really make a difference for you and your company.

And, equally important, the very best incubators aren't glorified coffee shops and co-working real estate plays; they are exceptional places that are purpose-built and run and managed every day to create a constant flood of educational opportunities, critical thoughts, game-changing ideas, new approaches and technologies which change and expand every day because new people are constantly moving in, moving up and/or moving out of the place. They may be growing or about to be going, but the one thing that's for sure is that they are spending every day just like you facing the same kinds of challenges, coming up with new and novel solutions, and suffering all the ups and downs of the startup process that we know and love so well. And you can learn more from them – their bumps and bruises – triumphs, trials and terrors - than from just about any other source.

You might argue that colleges and universities are equally fertile environments for this kind of energy and excitement, information exchanges and aggressive testing of new ideas, and rapid change, but you'd be dead wrong. Sadly, our bulk of our higher education system is about the repeated regurgitation of conventional wisdom and the creation of self-congratulatory dissertations which purport to validate "new" versions of old and tired news. While validation is really important in parking lots, it has very little to do with change, exploration or discovery. And concepts like commercialization, monetization and moving concepts from the labs (and sterile papers and articles) out into the real and very messy world where they can make a difference in people's lives are equally foreign ideas.

In addition, our universities lack just about everything that really matters to the process of disruptive business innovation and new company creation: (a) there's no existential requirement to get some customers and sell something because the professors will always have their jobs and their tenure; (b) there's no sense of urgency to make payroll because they always get a paycheck and there's always another quarter or semester around the corner with a fresh crop of anxious students; and frankly, and most unfortunately, (c) there's absolutely no reward structure in place at any of these places for the slightest risk-taking or for even thinking about making real changes in the way things have always been done. And if the sad combination of those things didn't suck all the juice, mojo and enthusiasm out of these places, it's also downright uncool at college for the "adults" to be passionate and excited about anything outside their academic ivory towers or to be seen as promoting or marketing just about anything. So it's just not happening at So What U.

On the other hand, in an incubator, if you're open to it, you learn by looking, listening and doing every day. This is because you get to free ride on three important trends that are driving rapid and radical change at light speed throughout the tech economy and even in more basic industries as well. Keep an eye out for these 3 drivers:

(1) <u>Solution Migration</u>

What's good for the goose is often just as good and helpful for the gander (except, I suppose, right around Thanksgiving time) and so we are seeing more and more instances where a quick and effective technology solution (or even one that took years and millions to develop and perfect) in one industry (like precision drug dosing cartridges) is ported and rapidly migrates to other industries (like self-service food and beverage providers) overnight and with just as much success and impact. Smart players in almost every major industry (except the U.S. government) have figured this out and are aggressively pursuing these kinds of parallel research and investigation programs. And they're also stepping up to invest in and buy more and more startups as M & A is rapidly becoming the new R & D.

(2) <u>Cross-Industry Pollination</u>

An entirely separate, but equally extensive area for lateral learning is more about behavioral benchmarks and expectations rather than technologies. Seeing what works socially in adjacent businesses; seeing what it's reasonable to ask of and expect from consumers these days and what the *quid pro quo* needs to be; understanding the new dimensions of self-service and constant connectivity; etc. are all inquiries and directions of investigation that are crucial components of how you bring your business to the new digital marketplaces. Just because we haven't previously expected customers to be responsive to certain changes in the way we do business or we have never before asked people to behave in certain new ways doesn't mean that these aren't very significant directions (and potentially opportunities for enormous savings) for your company. The trick here is to let someone else do the first round of experimenting and seeing what and whether anything blows up in their faces before you make your moves. Clearly, as a recent example, the Netflix debacle with Qwikster where they tried for two weeks to split their business into two distinct pieces and almost immediately lost hundreds of thousands of customers and millions of dollars kept a whole lot of other companies from jumping off a similar cliff with their pricing plans. It's always better to let the other guys make the first mover mistakes and then to be a smarter fast follower.

(3) <u>Inexpensive Adaptation</u>

It's not critical or essential that your version of a copied or borrowed solution be gold-plated or crazy expensive at the outset. Try it first with duct tape and chewing gum and see what happens before you bet the farm. You'll learn a lot, maybe you'll lose a little, but you'll never know what can work for you if you don't try. Just don't put both feet into the pond until you know how deep the water is.

Each of these approaches offers value and opportunities for your company as long as you spend the time to think about what they can bring to your business. Keep in mind that the power and value of a change isn't necessarily related to its size. Sometimes the most valuable and important aspect of these things isn't about how much you have to change to make a difference, but exactly how little a change needs to be to make a big impact.

STARTUPS SHOULDN'T SELL STRATEGY

In the "been there, done that" category of mistakes that you should only make once, I would award a place of high honor to the idea that startups should spend their scarce capital and limited resources trying to "earn" their way into the hearts and wallets of big customers by selling strategy as a door opener. By "strategy," I mean various attempts, presentations, mock-ups, etc. designed to show these big guys the disruptive and scary future and how your company can help them successfully navigate through the coming tough times for their businesses. Here's a flash – these attempts at show and tell (which are really just some smart guys showing off) almost never end well for the little guys – that's you – and, worse yet, it deflects your best people and a lot of your focus in the wrong direction.

I realize that there's an ego component to this stuff and also some bragging rights about who you're pitching and getting in front of. But egos aside, the bottom line is whether anyone is going to be writing you a check any time soon. The method doesn't work, the metrics are always muddled at best, and, for sure, the math is a killer because you rarely get paid anything for the privilege of spending your time chasing these guys. To be successful, you need to develop, design and incorporate your strategies and your solutions into your offerings rather than trying to use them as come-ons and commercials for how well you'll eventually do for the customers.

And, of course, the biggest and saddest joke in this formulation is the word "selling" because - in 99 cases out of 100 - startups aren't selling anything – they're really giving away their time, knowledge and insights for free. Some folks think of this approach as "bread on the water," but I'd say this isn't a loss leader or an intelligent marketing cost; for a startup, I'd say it's much more likely to be a business buster. You end up spending your precious time educating a bunch of folks who often turn out to be indifferent ingrates at the end of the process and politely tell you that (a) they've decided to do it themselves (which we all know that they can't do - even if they steal your ideas); (b) that they're gonna do it elsewhere; or – in many cases because of fear, inertia, or ignorance - that (c) they're not going to do it at all. And only you and your team are that much worse for the wear.

And – if that wasn't bad enough – you'll also learn quickly from your investors (after a couple of these expensive adventures go nowhere) that they thought they were buying into a product or service business and not a consulting firm. They don't want explorers and educators; they want executors. They don't want you strategizing; they want you selling. Fully engaged in turning your ideas into invoices. They're gonna tell you that they'd rather see a month of consistent singles and doubles than wait 3 months hoping for a home run which may never come. As a scrambling startup, you just can't afford that kind of investment.

So forget it. But just in case you can't resist the temptation or the bogus blandishments about how bright you are (think: "that hooker really liked me" in cases of self-delusion like this), here are a few things to keep in mind to help you avoid a total wipeout.

(1) Don't Get Pushed Around

The biggest bullies in big companies are the boys with the least actual power. They can say "No" all day long, but they can't say "Yes" and they know it. They couldn't greenlight a project if their life depended on it - unless it happened to cost a lot less than a latte. So they spend their time taking their frustrations out on you and tormenting young entrepreneurs who don't know any better with big empty promises of good things to come down the line. And – in the meantime – they're only asking for the sun, moon and stars – all for free – because that's pretty much all they've got to spend.

Here's the straight dope: you don't have to give away or prove anything to these guys because they don't matter. Find the folks who can actually sign a check and get in front of them. They're a lot easier to deal with and they can make a real deal happen. They're also a lot nicer too because they don't have a big chip on their shoulders. And they know that - if you want something of real value – you have to pay for it. If you pay peanuts, you get monkeys.

(2) Get Profitable First

Too many complimentary pitches and big bunches of brainstorming freebies will mean too little inbound cash flow and that means trouble for any startup. You need to have an aggressive containment strategy (a limited number of ongoing anythings and that's it) and you need to be sure that your sales team isn't taking the easy way out by selling air and getting paid nothing for it. It's not a "win" when all the commitments and all the costs are on your side of the table. The real focus of management needs to be on making sure that you are identifying and signing up paying customers. The size of the individual deals is nowhere near as critical as the cash. Another important bonus is that these deals don't take as long to launch or as long to complete as many of the bigger ones might.

The truth is that you simply can't afford to pass up the small fish while you're waiting for the whales. See http://www.inc.com/howard-tullman/why-small-wins-beat-big-ones.html. Big companies are one of the last refuges of the slow "No" and there's just about nothing worse for a startup than that. A fast rejection (it only hurts for a bit) is always better than being stroked and strung out by a guy who gets paid to have meetings rather than to make decisions and progress. Once you're making even a little money, you can consider whether to roll the dice on some bigger proposals. Don't be a hurry.

(3) Get A Pilot Project

Don't leave the conversation once you're in the room without something. A trial, a test, a pilot, a prototype, etc. These are all good ways to get the ball rolling, but not for nothing. And equally important you must make sure that there's a clear and express agreement on just what you're committing to do and what exactly will constitute success and the steps to follow afterwards. If the metrics and measurements aren't properly aligned and apparent, you're as likely as not to get to the end of the project and have nothing to show for it because you didn't get the right rules established at the outset.

And don't think that any agreement is better than no agreement because a bad beginning agreement can set the wrong tone for the whole relationship. And don't think that only newbies make these kinds of mistakes. *YouTube* and plenty of celebrities make $300 million worth of these mistakes just a little while ago. See http://www.inc.com/howard-tullman/three-lessons-from-youtubes-programming-disaster.html . So get something, but make sure you know what you're getting yourself into.

(4) Get Paid

If you don't ask, you don't get. You know what your stuff is worth (or you should) and you shouldn't be embarrassed to say that you stopped giving it away for free a while ago. We have all heard the stories about what great reference clients some of these companies will make for your business and these tales are basically BS because everyone in the industry who matters knows that the very same guys make a habit of never paying new companies anything for the chance to test their products or services. They never pick up the check and, after a little while, they start to lose respect for the companies that keep working for free. Just like the patsy in the poker game; if you don't know who it is after 30 minutes of playing (or too many free trials), it's you.

(5) <u>Get Partners Who Are Already in the Door</u>

There are a lot of big companies scared to death these days of everything digital and under tremendous pressure from their own customers and clients to figure things out in a hurry. This kind of demand would be encouraging overall except that these companies simply aren't built for speed in anything and that's where the opportunities are being created for clever young companies with the chops and the technology to get these kinds of jobs done quickly, relatively cheaply and - most importantly - quietly. Think of the big guys as today's Trojan Horses. They're already inside the walls – they have the relationships that would take you years to build with the biggest brands and players around – and they are hurting for help. They can make good partners and you can make them look good as long as you're careful to make sure that your IP and financial interests are protected and that they aren't selling you the same bill of goods about future fortunes that their clients will try to do.

"SMART REACH"
KEEPS GETTING SMARTER

I've been saying for a while now that the context in which you communicate with your customers is actually more important and material to the success of the communication than the content itself. Your pitch can be Hollywood-quality and utterly heroic, but it will only hit home with those who hear it. We want to be talking to the folks who are willing to listen (and maybe even interested in our story) and not to the accidental observers, the poor suckers who are duped into clicking on random crap, or the people who don't even see our offerings because they're positioned "below the fold" in digital terms. I pity the fools who are still paying millions of dollars for videos "shown", but not seen by any human beings. And I can't wait for the media agencies who are still selling clicks instead of real, measurable results to credulous cretins to take their last desperate breaths and disappear.

In addition, it's increasingly clear that the source of the information and the credibility and connection of the referring/sharing party matters more than brand, celebrity endorsements, bogus rankings, etc. This is precisely why social is rapidly overtaking search as the primary source of everything we want to know about and why Facebook continues to blow away Google on every possible scale. We want to hear from the people who we know and whose opinions we value and not from the crowd or a bunch of strangers with nothing better to do. In addition, people with broad connections and networks within their organizations or cohorts turn out to have just as much (or more) viral power and amplification capacity as the for-sale "influencers" that everyone has been chasing for the last several years. We just not as dumb any more as the dopes on Madison Avenue continue to think we are. We are looking for authentic, accurate, actionable and timely information to make our buying decisions and it has become a reasonable and realistic expectation that this is exactly what the best and most competitive businesses will provide.

We call this approach "smart reach" – what I want, when I want it, wherever I am, and without asking. And it keeps getting smarter as our data and our tools continue to improve. What has changed the game recently is that the degrees of possible precision in targeting have continued to become more particular, detailed and granular. It's simply no longer sufficient to use proxies, placeholders, and best guesses in order to properly target and reach your audience. In addition, just knowing who the audience is isn't enough information any longer to be the predicate for an effective communication strategy: you've got to know what they are interested in and – even more importantly – when – in terms of their behaviors – when to reach out to them in order to complete the circle.

There's a simple reason that high value products searches are almost all taking place these days on Amazon and not Google or other search engines. When I'm engaged in a defined activity, I go to the power tool for that job – the specialist, not the GP – because I'm time-constrained and I'm trying to get something specific done. I'm not browsing and I'm not bored – it's not a discover exercise, it's a task.

And it's in this mode that the more valuable assistance and offerings you can provide for me (including suggestive selling and "nudge" commerce ideas), the more real value you are providing and the more receptive I am to the pitch. This seems pretty obvious and simple – you're being helpful and additive – not distracting or irrelevant. But it's a message that being missed by the masses of marketers at the moment. If you don't incorporate the mode of my behavior into your marketing model, you're missing the boat.

There's an interesting debate developing right now that addresses exactly these kinds of concerns. It has to do with the fact that – while Facebook has now caught up with (and possibly passed) YouTube in terms of the number of video views per day (call it 4 billion plus a day for each of them) – YouTube argues that the engagement levels of the viewers with each YouTube video are dramatically different and much more substantial and that this "context" makes YouTube a much more attractive channel for video ad placements. YouTube says that Facebook's video "views" suffer from all the same complaints I mentioned above – inadvertent views, distracted viewers, drive-bys, etc. – and that – as a result – the appropriate context for delivering the right video ad to an interested viewer isn't present. But, of course, when the videos you're being shown are sent by your friends and are actually theoretically meaningful to you, you could argue just the opposite - that I'm more likely to watch and be interested and receptive to related video content in this mode – than when I'm bored and scrolling thru random video recommendations on YouTube hoping to find the next great cat video.

In any case, the more major takeaway is that we do many materially different things when we're online (and also we behave differently when we're mobile – which almost everyone is these days – as opposed to when we're sitting in front of a screen) and our attitudes and receptivity to messaging varies as well. In order to reach us effectively, you've got to know how to determine and your plan needs to take into account that my interest in your message will vary greatly depending on whether I'm shopping, gaming, socializing, or just scrolling. Messages that aid and assist me in the process are welcomed – things that interrupt or are irrelevant are ignored.

So the bottom line is pretty simple: if your audience isn't listening, it doesn't matter what you are saying or how well you are saying it. The right pitch at the right point in time and place is the only message that matters and the only one that will make it thru the confusion and the clutter to the customer.

3 THINGS STARBUCKS IS DOING REALLY RIGHT

I had a conversation with a commodities trader recently about Starbucks and how their results have been so impressive over the last year or two. He said that the main reason the stock had done so well was that they were enjoying the financial advantages of depressed commodity prices for coffee. He thought their recent growth was all about their cost structure which frankly – in his opinion - was more a matter of great good luck than anything that they had actively done to manage for this outcome or to achieve these results. I guess when you're a hammer, everything looks like a nail.

I told him that he was totally missing the boat and looking at the wrong metrics and that – because his perspective was off - he wasn't giving the company and their management team anywhere near the credit that they deserved. Interestingly enough, we're drowning in data today, but the sheer increase in available information isn't improving our analytical abilities or helping us (as much as it should) to make better decisions. You can be so focused on particular numbers that it's easy to lose sight of the bigger picture. We think we know what's going on and why, but - on closer examination - it turns out that we're looking in the wrong direction or commending or complaining to our managers about things that are often beyond their control.

Just because some things may look differently these days doesn't mean that anything has actually changed. The bottom line of any good business still grows because its revenues are increased (without an offsetting rise in operating expenses) or because its costs are materially reduced without any sacrifice in the level of its sales. This is the immutable math of margins and it has been ever thus. Nonetheless, it's surprising how often confusion sneaks into this basic equation, alters the correct calculations, and results in inaccurate causal attribution. It may be math, but it's got to be good math and the right metrics to matter.

And even the sharpest managers are guilty of applying versions of the same faulty logic and erroneous explanations - especially when it's in their near-term best interests to do so. In good earnings periods, they're more than happy to take plenty of credit for benefits beyond their bailiwick and in tough times they're pretty quick to blame poor outcomes on bad actors and external forces. I remember when I was selling my computerized resume service to colleges that, in good economic times, the schools bragged on their "job placement" centers, but, in hard times, those same folks took to calling themselves "career guidance" counselors. Actual jobs weren't any longer a part of their jurisdiction.

A lot of this is just human nature, but when you start focusing on or blaming third parties and outside events for your successes or your difficulties, you give up the power to make the kinds of changes which are necessary to continue to improve the situation. Similarly, when you're looking in all the wrong locations for the explanations; you're never going to end up in the right place. The most important job is to illuminate the correct causes so you can eliminate the real problems and so you can also accelerate your commitments to and investments in the things that are actually moving your business forward.

In our conversation, I went on to say, just for starters, that Starbucks had recently raised their prices and that – notwithstanding the sticker shock (as if anyone really noticed or cared except the press) - their customer counts (and, of course, their top line revenues) were still growing. They weren't trying to save their way to success. (See http://www.inc.com/howard-tullman/saving-your-way-to-success-why-you-cant-do-it.html). Frankly, if you're going to take advantage of improved operating efficiencies or available short-term cost savings due to market movements, the smart play is generally to pass those savings on to your customers by reducing your prices to draw more customers in, not to jack your prices up and try to soak the current group. This is the approach which Walmart and Costco have clearly mastered.

And yet, Starbucks seems at the moment to have the best of both worlds. I told my trader buddy that there had to be a better explanation than commodity costs for the kind of pricing power (and price elasticity) that Starbucks continues to demonstrate. My view was that what was improving their overall results was a series of initiatives that the company continued to aggressively advance and that the commodity cost savings were simply additive to, not dispositive of, their overall earnings momentum.

I felt that there were 3 areas where they were just hitting it out of the park and that these were the kind of long-term growth drivers that were driving the continuing appreciation in the Starbucks stock price as well. These are some of the same levers and tools that every startup can also use and which every one of them needs to be addressing as early as possible in their own growth plans.

First, I said that I was impressed with the fact that the number of participants in the Starbucks reward program has grown to over 10 million people and that these "members" spent on average 3 times as much as non-members do. There is nothing better for the bottom line than growing the average ticket of your existing customers. (See http://www.inc.com/howard-tullman/why-knocking-on-old-doors-is-the-best-sales-strategy.html). They're already inside the tent and now you've just got to show them more attractive opportunities to increase their spend with you while they're there. Virtually no marketing costs and a direct benefit to the bottom line. And loyalty programs continue to pay multiple dividends beyond straight dollars – they drive powerful word of mouth, authentic endorsements, community growth, social media amplification, etc. Every new startup from Day One needs to understand that building a real business is about capturing and retaining the lifetime value of each of those customers which you spend big (and scarce) bucks to acquire and that membership is about much more than just privileges, it's critical to profits as well.

Second, purchases thru the Starbucks mobile app are now accounting for more than 20% of the daily in-store sales. Saves time, saves personnel costs, improves speed and satisfaction – what's not to love? Starbucks (and many other retailers) are rapidly heading in the direction of having their products ready and waiting for you to pick up rather than having you wait for the stuff once you get there. And, of course, it's all about connectivity and mobility. In Europe, the hottest trend ("click and pick") is to order online and then drive to the store to pick up your purchases – often from a drive-thru window. But incorporating a viable mobile solution into your order fulfillment and payment streams isn't as easy as it seems either inside your company (for obvious legacy and enterprise-wide issues) or, more importantly, outside of your company's four walls because it's VERY tough to get the typical consumer these days to add any proprietary app to their already crowded and cluttered phones. You've got to show them a really good reason or try to figure out how to fold your functions into an app that's already there. (See http://www.inc.com/howard-tullman/want-your-app-to-succeed-get-it-out-there.html). This is why Starbucks has such a leg up (with 10 million rewards members) on businesses like McDonald's, for example, who's just trying to get into the game and doesn't really understand the major barriers to adoption which they're facing. The truth is that no one these days really needs another app.

And third, Starbucks keeps adding new complementary products and services offered by on-brand channel partners (NY Times, Spotify, Lyft, etc.) who are dying to get at their affluent and highly-consumptive customers. Having made the acquisition investment, this is a great way to amortize some of their sunk and ongoing costs and still keep growing the overall pie at the same time. It's a lot easier (and much less costly and risky) for third parties to pay Starbucks for this access than it is for them to try to lay their own pipe and reach all of these customers themselves. If the bundles are well done, they can clearly benefit both marketing parties and the consumer. Any business that can become the go-to channel for already assembled concentrations of ready-to-buy customers is in exactly the right place these days to reap the rewards that inure to the gatekeepers and toll takers sitting astride the mobile web. But, here again, you have to be careful that the experience is additive and appreciated by the customers or it's not worth the incremental revenue for your business.

Everything today is about the overall experience and trying to add too much to the process can be a real buzz kill as well as a persistent problem especially when nothing matters more to the customer than getting in and getting out of the place as fast as possible. I want to grab a Venti and vamoose! There's a lot to love about that dolce latte; but my time's much more valuable than your caffe mocha.

MAKE ME CARE AND
THEN I'LL SHARE

I have been talking for a while now about an important distinction between the content (message) of an attempted communication and the context (channel and timing) in which that content is delivered. The main objective of smart marketing is to successfully engage the customers/consumers at the right time in a useful dialogue, which has become increasingly two-way and interactive, and not to engulf them in a continual and indiscriminate flood of inappropriate and irrelevant material.

If you get all the elements correct (right time, right place, and right message), you're golden. If you blow it, it means nothing but grief for all concerned. And yet, this basic idea apparently hasn't dawned on millions of marketers who just keep mechanically shoveling their shit our way and who think that there's still some value in sheer velocity and volume. They're dead wrong; they're consistently antagonizing and alienating their audiences; they'll eventually be barred and shut off from these channels, and their clients and companies are paying a heavy price for their ignorance. If they don't quickly change their rationale, their approach and their direction, they'll be left in the dust.

The truth these days is that – given the noise, the clutter and the fierce competition for our fleeting and precious attention – the basic rule of thumb is quite simple: if I'm not listening, it doesn't matter what you're saying. You should save your breath and your bullets for smarter, better and more cost-effective targets. I have previously called this approach the need to focus on "smart reach" and you can catch up on the concept here: http://www.inc.com/howard-tullman/to-sell-more-your-marketing-must-embrace-smart-reach.html. Basically, you've got to provide each customer with what he or she wants, when he or she wants it, wherever he or she is, and without asking. Otherwise, all bets are off.

But the idea of "smart reach" alone is yesterday's news for those of us who are focused on keeping ahead of the game as well as the competition. The expectations of the consumer are ever changing and progressive (constantly rising). We all know that what may have worked well for us in the past (and, in fact, most of our prior experiences and successes) aren't likely to be relevant to creating tomorrow's triumphs. Just doing the same old things isn't going to make for better results – especially as the competition all around us continues to mount. Experience, in times of radical disruption and change, can be much more of an albatross, a constraint, and a problem for growing businesses rather than something they can comfortably rely upon. See http://www.inc.com/howard-tullman/navigating-the-information-superhighway. html . And so the moving finger keeps writing new stories and it's those new stories that will create and build the critical connections to the consumer in the future.

And, as smart and aggressive a focus on "smart reach" still may be for many businesses that haven't even begun to advance their thinking; I'm afraid that the bar is jumping up again and that smart reach's time has come and gone as a "be-all, end-all" strategy. This is in part because it's a uni-directional concept (a remnant of the old broadcast "one-to-many" era rather than reflective of our new networked economy) and that's no longer the two-way world we have to operate in. Today all 3 of the main nightly network news broadcasts reach only about 22 million viewers while every day more than 160 million people in the U.S. check in with Facebook. This is the new "many-to-many" environment in which we learn as much or more laterally from our peers as we do from any top-down sources.

Smart reach is all about customized mass communication and individualized messaging, but today we need to think more about our interactions with the customers and consumers as multi-directional conversations: conversations with us, discussions and interactions between interest groups, and third-party sharing among consumers and their peers and influencers as well - in which we will never be direct participants. We know that we couldn't be everywhere the consumer is today even if we tried. And we also acknowledge that we can't service and control every channel to the consumer even with unlimited time and resources. But being there when the buyer is ready to buy is the most critical objective of all. If you can't be found, you will never be chosen.

So the best new strategies have a lot more to do with conversations than simple communications and a lot more to do with advocates and influencers than with advertising and infomercials. This isn't easy for a lot of folks to swallow, no good marketer ever wants to trust his or her fate to others and give up some degree of control over the messaging, but it's easier than you might imagine once you understand that it's no longer about you or your products and services – it's all about them. It's their agenda, they want to drive the process, and you need to figure at least how you can hitch a ride.

If we can't be there ourselves (directly or indirectly), and that's increasingly a given, when these critical conversations and decisions are taking place, then we need to have our messages convincingly and consistently carried forth by authentic and motivated messengers – prompted (but not paid) proxies if you will – who will make it their mission to passionately promote our products and services. Make them care – create a dream that they can adopt and make their own – and let them go forth and spread the word.

Consumers today don't really care to hear anything more about the features and attributes of your products; they want to know how those products will directly benefit them (value) and how they will make a difference in their day-to-day lives (impact). Today we trade our attention for offerings which we believe to have real and specific value for us. Just adding more information to the conversation has no intrinsic value unless it is (a) effectively and credibly communicated, (b) resonates with the target audience, and ultimately (c) impacts and drives the desired behaviors. If you can't make me care about what you have to say, I'll quickly move on to the next best thing. I call this the "show me or see ya" problem.

We really don't have the time or the inclination to do the heavy lifting of learning about new things or ideas these days, but we are willing to briefly listen. And who exactly do we listen to? Some things (like word of mouth) never change and we're still taking the lion's share of the guidance we seek on product and service selections from our friends and peers. But our universe of "friends" has expanded dramatically (and mainly artificially) to include a lot of influencers and others whose opinions and ideas we've come to trust and value even though they would never meet the traditional definition of a friend. Brands used to serve this purpose – as shorthand for quality, value, safety and reliability – but now – given the limited time we all have and the vast amount of choices and the frightening lack of quality decision-making data - we look to loudmouths (not in the pejorative sense), mavens and other mock and manufactured experts to tell us what they think we ought to know. And realistically, to reach these new audiences, these are the folks that you want to deliver your messages for you. And keep in mind that these aren't - by and large – hired guns, flacks, media people or celebrities; they're the ordinary, feet-on-the-street, every day denizens of the web, who are living the new technologies every day, and who the crowd has selected, endorsed and designated as the ones worth listening to.

These folks are a curious breed – passionate about being in the know – passionate about being ahead of the crowd – and most passionate about being in front of a crowd at all times. They live by the doctrine that nothing is real until you've shared it and that everything is better when it's shared. For some it's mostly ego, for some it's a desire to educate, and for the truest believers, it's an almost moral obligation that they feel to share something that has benefitted them with the masses. This is largely their lives (it's definitely <u>not</u> about the money) and they are at it as close to 24/7 as they can possibly be. Here again, in today's short-cycle world, you need people feeding the beast 24/7 on your behalf and these are the ones who seemingly can't help doing just that and couldn't stop doing it if they tried. I call them WOMbots. Word of Mouth "robots". And as peculiar and different as they may seem to us at the moment; they're a lot more likely to have both an immediate and a lasting impact on your business and our future than all the old-line ad agencies and all the new-line social media marketing businesses combined.

CRITICAL MASS VS CENTRIFUGAL FORCE

Starting and growing a new business has much more in common with a tornado (and some would say a marriage) than you might expect at first glance. They both begin with a lot of sucking and blowing and, if you're not careful and lucky as well, you could end up losing the house. And while it's never a good idea to bet against Mother Nature or gravity, the good news is that many of the things which are most likely to bring your business down are man-made and sometimes the product of your own actions or – more likely – inactions.

It's increasingly clear that the costs today of true inaction far outweigh the risks of just about anything you're willing to try to do. Keep in mind though that refusing to do things cheaply or quickly or too broadly or before you're fully prepared isn't inaction – it's good decision-making. The things you say "no" to - in the long run - will have a far greater favorable impact on your ultimate success than any quick hits or shortcuts you get sucked into pursuing before you're ready or it's time. Two easy ideas to keep top of mind: don't say "maybe" when you should say "no" and don't try to do something cheaply that you shouldn't do at all.

In addition, these days everyone is an expert on everything and a million people are willing to give you advice – especially when they have no responsibility or liability for the outcomes. (See http://www.inc.com/howard-tullman/expert-advice-is-overrated. html .) Their advice almost always sounds the same: "do something now"; "go big or go home"; "if you snooze, you lose"; "be the first mover", etc. But sometimes the best decision you can make is to say "no" and that's not because you don't want to act – it's because you want to act when and how you choose and when the time is right. It's not always the popular choice or decision, but it's almost always the smart one.

There are certainly going to be some unavoidable risks and existential threats to your company that you'll need to respond to and you're not going to end up anywhere worth going if you try to keep your head in the sand and just creep carefully forward. Things are just moving too rapidly in the global marketplace to act defensively and a go-slow strategy of risk avoidance can be a death sentence for a startup.

But, at the same time, there are also some bumps in the road and some obvious pressures and problems that you can sidestep if you keep your eyes open, pay attention to the signs, and know where to look. The trick is not to let any of these influences (the need for speed, the gospel of scale, the ecstasy of expansion, etc.) and/or influencers (analysts' and media's musings, competitors' and critics' complaints, investors' own agendas, politicians pushing for publicity, etc.) pull your business apart. Screw up your courage, stick to your guns, do what's right for the present, and be ready to flex in the future.

It's really a simple matter of physics. Critical mass actually is critical and it's your job to build or assemble it and to hang on to it. You're pulling everything – all the time – toward the center of things (you're a centripetal "force" – focused, attentive, deeply involved, etc.) trying to hold a lot of things together and the outside (and sometimes the inside) world is constantly conspiring to pull things away from you (they're centrifugal forces – "trying too much too soon", "spreading yourself a mile wide and an inch deep", "trying to be all things to all people", etc.). But as any good entrepreneur knows in his or her heart, you can't have it all. So the trick is to not get tricked into trying.

While many of these concerns are external and market- or competitor-driven, the most insidious ones are from the folks you think are your friends and who technically should be looking out for your best interests. Here's a flash – if they're human and they're breathing, they're looking out for their own interests first. That's just human nature and not a bad thing per se, it's just something to keep in mind as you consider their suggestions and thoughts. A grain or two of salt doesn't just make the soup tastier.

Influencers come in several recurring types, sizes and shapes – watch out for these:

(1) <u>VCs and Aggressive Investors</u>

Most of these guys never met a farm they wouldn't bet and your business (in their minds) is no different. Full speed ahead is the only speed they're interested in and, if you don't make it, they'll be long gone when the layoffs begin. Only moonshots matter and being in the middle of anything is mediocre at best and boring which is even worse. You're trying to build a firm foundation for a sustainable and profitable business and they're trying to find stories they can promote and sell to the next round of greater fools. It's not easy to tell these people to cool their jets from time to time and that your pace doesn't reflect the depth of your passion or your commitment. The best advice I can give you is to try to make sure that you've got some Board members and other advisors (not investors) who've actually run businesses to help take your side in some of the silliest of these arguments. They can help you push back. (See http://www.inc.com/howard-tullman/why-its-better-when-board-members-back-off.html .)

(2) Politicians

Politicians also love big winners, but they love patronage more and so their primary goals are favorable publicity (no surprise) and spreading the wealth around. As soon as they see a roaring success in the city, they want to put you and your business on the road and have you build copies and clones throughout the state or the country – whether it makes the slightest sense for you to do so or not – because their focus isn't on your progress, prosperity or profits, it's on the populace at large and they see it as the more sites and stories, the merrier. This is a great way to over-extend your business and end up spread so thin that nothing works anywhere and then – of course – it's gonna be shame on you when it all comes tumbling down and they'll be over the next hill chasing the newest shiny story. Rapid expansion is always exciting until it isn't and it's looks easy to everyone who doesn't have to execute the plan.

(3) Media

The media operate on a simple principle – they'll love ya 'til they don't and they're always waiting for you to slip on that banana peel and take a tumble. I realize that they're a necessary evil, but you need to be very careful that you're not saying things or doing things (even worse) to "prove" something to these people because (a) it's never enough to satisfy them in any case and they won't believe you anyway; and (b) it's a fool's errand to waste your time trying to impress people whose livelihood is much more about finding the warts and shortcomings in your story than in celebrating your successes. The best thing I can say about your interactions with most of the media today is the advice I heard long ago about why it makes no sense to wrestle with a pig. Only the pig enjoys it and you just eventually end up covered in mud.

The bottom line is simple: these are all distractions that do next to nothing for your business and are best avoided as much as humanly possible. Keep your head down, keep your eyes on the prize, keep moving forward and all the rest of this stuff will take care of itself if and when it matters at all.

PART II

CUSTOMER ACQUISITION & RETENTION

HELP YOUR CUSTOMERS
DO THEIR HOMEWORK

There are a lot of reasons why a prospect might make a first purchase from your company. Novelty, curiosity, lack of time to shop for or lack of knowledge about alternatives, pity or sympathy, effective PR and press, inexperience on their part, discounted initial pricing, great-looking marketing materials, fear of being left behind (the bandwagon effect) or shut out entirely (the scarcity argument), family or other connections or relationships, etc.

So, before you celebrate those early sales; drink the company Kool-Aid; or pat yourself too often on the back, take another careful look at the list. You'll notice that not a single cause or consideration really has anything to do with the quality of your product or service, the value of it to the user, or any of the other real-world measurements that matter in the long run. That's why first sales are easy compared to renewals where (for better or worse) you're dealing with an experienced customer and where nine times out of ten you're not even in the room (much less in the conversation) when the critical decisions are made about contract renewals or additional product purchases. It's this "second sale" (renewals or reorders) that secures the customer and cements the relationship for the long term.

And yet, way too many businesses take their customers for granted and then they're caught flat-footed and surprised when the customer quits or leaves. This is why – at all of my businesses – everyone understood for the day they started that renewals were just business, but that we took terminations personally. A termination was a slap in the face. Being "fired" by a customer was a kick in the teeth. And there was never anyone to blame except yourself because most terminations are entirely avoidable if you plan ahead and if you learn to do your customers' homework for them.

The first thing to keep in mind when you're trying to prevent customer attrition is that the guy who makes the renewal decision isn't usually the original buyer. He might consult with the first buyer, but, in general, he's a financial guy or an owner/check signer who's always looking to cut costs , reduce outlays, and to get rid of orphaned programs, services or subscriptions that no one uses any longer.

How does he know that no one is using some product or service? Here's the bad news – he doesn't have a clue and he doesn't really care. Because, in the absence of an advocate/champion within the business, the bean counter's rule is always to cut or cancel first and ask questions or apologize only after the screaming or complaining starts. And, since he guesses right so many times, he's pretty fearless. After all, it's not his ox that's getting gored, it's yours. And you don't even know the guy's name. He also knows that these days no one in the company really wants to be the person standing up and arguing for spending more money.

So how do you fight the invisible man who's about to cut off your oxygen and dump your product or service? Three little words: anticipation, preparation and ammunition.

Anticipation means knowing well in advance that a renewal is coming up and getting your licks in early and often. Any organization without a comprehensive renewal tracking and tickler system deserves to be run out of business and will be soon enough. One of the great innovations in this area was a system that American Hospital Supply developed to automatically re-stock the supply closets at the hospitals which were their customers. Their pitch was that this was just a handy way to make sure that no one was ever out of life-saving materials when they were needed, but the real beauty of the program was that it made it impossible for competitors to even get a foot in the door to sell their products since the supply closets were always full.

Preparation means taking the time to identify and recruit an internal champion – someone who works for the customer and whose job/life is made easier, smoother, or more profitable by using your product or service. Ideally, this person has the boss's ear or is the bean counter's buddy. He's your man in the back room who'll make your case when it's renewal time because it's also in his selfish interest to do that. But he can't do it alone or just using his wits and good looks. He's gonna need help.

Ammunition is the help he needs. It's the analysis, the back-up, the homework that you do for him so that he's prepared and equipped to make your case and justify the renewal. Sometimes it's a spreadsheet; sometimes it's a couple of case studies; or a prop and sometimes it's a market/competitive analysis that shows how your product or service is helping to make/keep his business a market leader. These things take time and they don't happen by themselves, but they make all the difference in the world because metrics and measurements mean everything today and the guy with the black and white goods is the guy who gets the gold. Happy talk and generalities are no match for solid math showing dollar and cents results. And even the bean counters back off when you've got the facts and figures on your side.

One of the simplest and most effective props I ever made was for our customer satisfaction research business in the automotive industry. It turns out that, even though it seems obvious to all of us that treating your customers better will lead to happier customers and a more profitable business, in the car business, it's been hard for the manufacturers to directly connect improved CSI scores (customer satisfaction index) with increased profits because the most profitable dealers are often the highest volume dealers and in many cases their service departments and after-sales activities suck because they're primarily in the business of pushing as many cars out the door as they can.

So I needed a way to demonstrate to a bunch of car guys who were buying my research services (following up with customers to make sure they were happy campers, etc.) that the cost of the service were modest compared to the added profits they'd be making if they improved their CSI scores. I hired a professor or two and had them build me a formula that linked improved customer satisfaction to increased profits, but I knew that their fancy math wasn't going to get the job done. So I built a little sliding calculator that let the dealers see in black & white exactly how much in additional profits each incremental improvement in their CSI score would mean to them. All they had to do was slide the little card up and down and the profits were virtually in the bag. Here's the slider:

 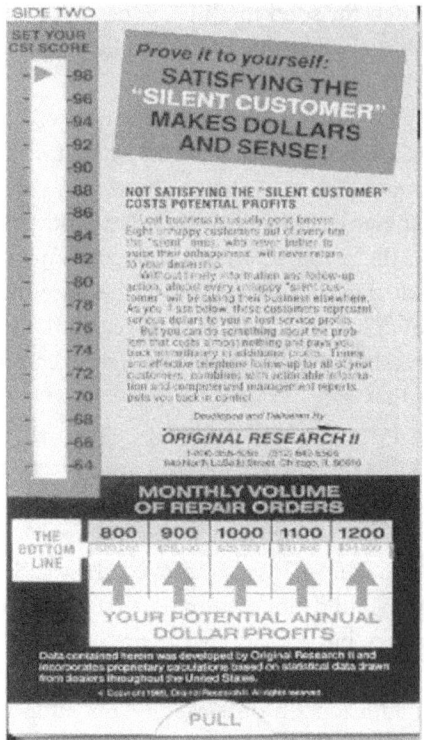

Was it accurate? I sure hope so. Did it work like a charm? You betcha. And why? Because we did their homework for them and gave it to them all wrapped up in a handy-dandy little "machine" to show their bosses and their bean counters.

And sometimes, that's all it takes to avoid those really ugly meetings and phone calls where the client quits. A little thought, a 50-cent prop that buys you thousands of dollars of business, and some basic salesmanship.

Anticipation, preparation and ammunition are the keys to owning your customers for a lifetime.

CUSTOMER EXPECTATIONS ARE PROGRESSIVE

Time has a nasty way of turning even your best assets into liabilities and even your happiest customers have a way of taking yesterday's "miracles" for granted (or worse – thinking that your products and services are old and tired) and looking elsewhere. They're always looking for the next new thing and the news media and the competition conspire regularly to stoke these desires for novelty and change.

If you're there to respond to these ever-expanding requirements and demands, you have a good chance of holding your own. But that's about it. On the other hand, if you want to grow your business, you need to anticipate these new consumer demands – not simply react to them – and you need a plan and a program to consistently get out ahead of your customers. Relationships that don't move forward and improve consistently deteriorate. One day, you turn around and the customer is gone. And by and large they don't give you any real warning; they don't generally complain; and they certainly don't ask your permission. They just disappear.

If you aren't aggressively watching your business and your customers and your competition, this situation won't be a problem for too long because you won't have any business to worry about. Suffice it to say, you can't sell anything sitting on your seat and you can't learn anything with actively and consistently listening to and for your customers. As you'll see, even when we try to listen, we often miss the main messages because we tend to listen primarily for what we want to hear – not what we need to hear.

Here's a quick example about doctors – some of the worst listeners in the world. One of my earliest businesses was Original Research II and our job was to measure customer satisfaction across many different industries. We were asked by a very large group of doctors to determine what considerations were most important to their patients and prospective patients. At the same time, we also polled all of the doctors in the practice to determine what they believed were the main drivers for patients. The results were fascinating and frightening.

Patients' Actual Priorities	Doctors' Presumed Drivers
Location	Specialty
Office Hours	Board Certifications
Free and Convenient Parking	Technical Skills
Insurance Coverage	Referrals - Word of Mouth
A Great Receptionist	Insurance Coverage

Needless to say, these results were the rudest of awakenings for the doctors. It was absolutely clear that a concerned and considerate staff was WAY more important than the most highly-trained surgeon on the team.

We did a similar project for bank officers and compared what they felt were important considerations for their customers to the customers' actual concerns and the primary causes for customer defections. There were a number of issues, but the overwhelming disconnect was that more than 67% of the customers felt that inattention was the worst possible sin and the largest problem – they could live with everything else – but when they came to believe that no one was paying attention to them, they stopped caring and left.

The bank officers, on the other hand, were largely consumed by mechanical and procedural considerations like price, interest rates, errors, credit decisions and paid only scant attention to the fundamental emotional consideration and customer desire of being appreciated and wanted. The only thing that we could say in their defense is that it was probably true that their primary interactions with the customers related to these process issues and that the customers probably felt uncomfortable expressing to anyone their personal feelings about how they believed the bank treated and regarded them. No one wants to be a number.

But here's the really sad part of this story. Failing to connect, cultivate and extend your relationships with your existing customers means that you are forfeiting the opportunity to harvest the easiest and most cost-effective additional profits available to any business. Spending time and money to find new customers (conquest marketing) is OK, but deepening your involvement with your current customers and increasing their average spend as well as locking them in for life (relationship marketing) is the brass ring.

KNOCK ON OLD DOORS

Failing to connect and cultivate your existing customers means that you are missing the chance to grab some easy incremental profits. Deepening your involvement with your current customers and increasing their average spend as well as locking them in for life (relationship marketing) is the real key to building an increasingly valuable business.

I call this strategy "knocking on old doors" because these customers are already in the tent (which means there are no new acquisition costs) and you're already touching them (hopefully on a consistent basis) so now you simply have to up the ante and the incentives and you'll see some amazing results. And, by the way, upping the ante and improving your connections with these current customers doesn't have to cost you a dime more – it's usually just a matter of attention and focus.

Instead of spending money chasing new customers (conquest marketing) or trying to steal customers from the competition (often by competing on price – which is a bad thing to do any time), you should stick to your knitting and direct your energies and your efforts to the lowest-hanging fruit – the people you're already doing business with. Just do a better job of that and they will take care of the rest.

The other equally wasteful activity is to spend too much time fretting about why customers who do leave left. It hurts, of course, to lose any customers (especially when you're small), but when you do the math, you quickly discover that customer defections (unforced by errors) account for a few percentage points of total revenue – an amount that can quickly and exponentially be offset by redirecting the same funds and resources used in the "why'd they go" exercise to engaging more deeply and meaningfully with the next higher tier of remaining customers which is always a much larger and more valuable population. A small overall improvement in this pool of customers will mean a lot more economically than trying to chase a few people who've left.

And if that math doesn't convince you in and of itself, here's the closer from one consumer survey we did for our large banking customers. More than 55 percent of customer defections on an annual basis were caused by two uncontrollable and unavoidable events - death and job transfers or other geographic relocations. All the fretting in the world won't keep the family in town if father's new job or position is halfway across the country.

None of this is rocket science – it's just common sense. Happy, "cared-for" customers spend more. And "organic" customers (basically home-grown) spend LOTS more than customers acquired through one-off marketing spends, promotions, and other incentives that may attract incremental customers, but don't create lasting connections to them. And sometimes customers leave you for reasons beyond your control. But what you may not realize is that the happy customers who stay with you also boost your business and your profits in a multitude of other ways. Here are some of the basic ways that your customers increase your profits when you "knock on old doors":

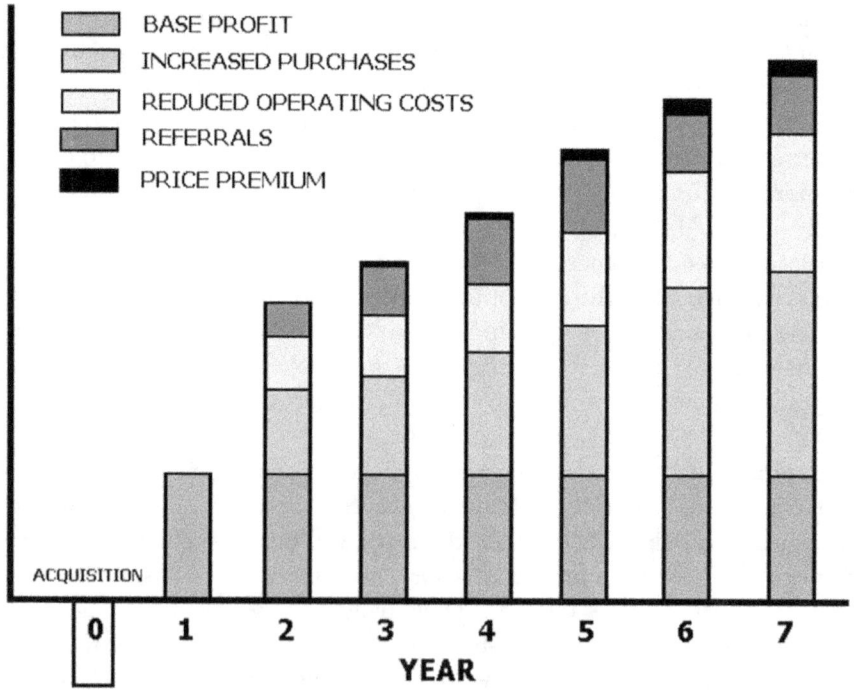

Yep, it's a fact. You can even charge your happiest customers <u>more</u> for certain types of status and premium offerings and they will stand in line to pay the tab. And they'll bring their friends, family and co-workers as well. So, the bottom line is that the care and feeding of your customers is even more important and valuable to your business than you imagined.

Constantly migrating your customers up the spending curve needs to be an on-going part of your marketing strategy even though it's technically "internal" marketing and, for that reason, it often gets overlooked or pushed aside. But if you want to "own" your customers for life, great service, careful listening and continual customer maintenance are crucial.

CLOSE THE BACK DOOR

I t's more important to deepen your connection to your existing customers than to spend a lot of time and money trying to figure out why certain customers left. After all, while you might learn some things from the process, you can't really water yesterday's crops and, in any case, it feels a little too much to me like crying over spilt milk. Extract the necessary lessons, fix what can be fixed, and move forward.

But that's not to say that you shouldn't care about losing customers. Nothing is more important to your bottom line than preventing customer attrition and avoiding churn. I'm just saying that, once they're gone, they're pretty much gone so the real key is to hang on to them by "closing the back door". If you can't do this, and you're spending a fortune on the front end to pull in new customers while you're losing them out the back, your company's going nowhere fast. It's like kissing your sister or as Yogi Berra used to say about his road trips: "We're lost, but we're making good time." The truth is that, if you're losing customers as quickly as you adding them, you're not making or building anything – you're just treading water – and once you run out of money, they make you go home.

The name of the long and winning game is to "own" your customers for life and to anticipate, meet and, in fact, try to exceed their needs and their expectations throughout your relationship with them. The key word is "anticipate" and the biggest change in all businesses today is that we now have the tools and the data concerning virtually all of our customers that should permit us to totally manage our relationships with them if we invest the time and money to look at the available information and – most importantly – if we know what we are looking for.

Everything in life happens on a continuum (or a series of cycles) and your job is to monitor your customers' timelines and jump in at the appropriate junctures (long before the competition is even in the game) to make the next connection and the next sales.

This approach is equally true whether you <u>think</u> you are selling a product or a service. The smartest operators know that every business is really a service business today because the real nature of every business is that it's always about making the next sale, managing the next interaction or event, delivering an uninterrupted stream of service, etc. You never want the customer "to come up for air" because if he or she does re-enter the marketplace and starts shopping around, your job becomes a million times harder.

So the real task and the critical questions are always the same – how do I know when to act and how do I pre-empt/intercept the customer at exactly the right times in our relationship? The answer is actually easier than you would think because - even though the start and stop points on the cycle may vary by customer - at some definable and determinable point, every customer will move through the same cycle. You just have to understand and learn how to measure and manage the cycles.

Here's the most valuable chart you will ever see. Keep in mind that it not only applies to the customers in your business; it also applies to your current relationship or marriage and to every other significant connection you will ever have with other human beings. So use it early and often because it describes the critical cycle of consumption that governs our interaction with everything we love and value.

THE CYCLE OF CONSUMPTION

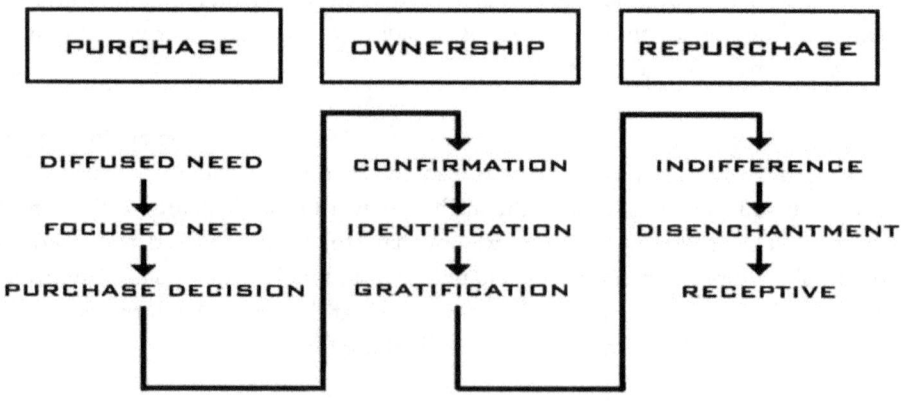

The "trick" as you might imagine is to consistently get your next "offer" in front of the customer somewhere right before DISENHANCEMENT so that you glide into RECEPTIVE as the only horse in town.

The chart below illustrates a more practical view of a consumption cycle that relates to the point in time (the "CROSSOVER POINT") when the remaining value of a consumer's car exceeds the amount of the loan balance which the consumer still owes on that car. From the standpoint of an automobile dealer, this is the ideal time to make a new offer to the consumer which basically amounts to a proposal to turn in his or her old car; get a brand-new car; and get a brand-new 48-60 month loan repayment book to go along with it.

Why is this a compelling offer for the customer? Because in virtually every case, the customer can be told that his monthly payments will remain the same EVEN THOUGH he or she will be driving a brand-new car. In addition, there's no car salesman to deal with; no time wasted negotiating; no anxiety about getting a fair deal or a fair trade-in; and, of course, from the dealer's standpoint, there's no competition.

THE ROAD TO REPURCHASE

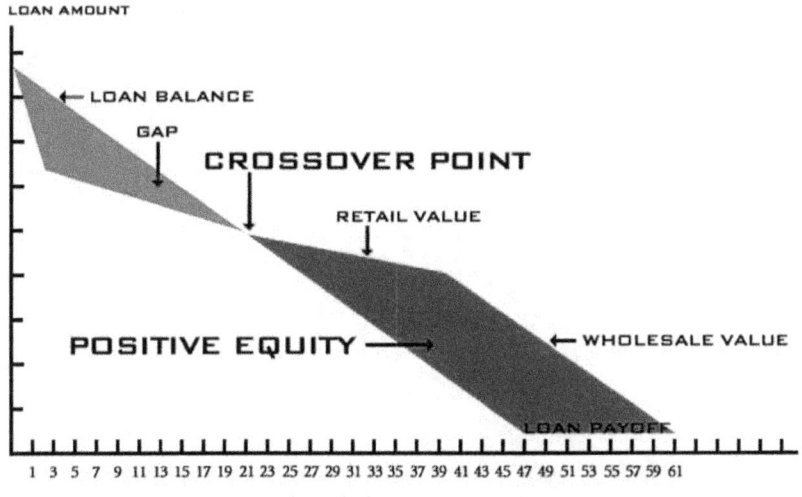

Now the cycles are going to vary dramatically depending on a variety of important considerations and they will vary from industry to industry as well. Some of the variables which will impact the types and durations of the cycles (but not the fundamental stages or phase within the cycle) include: (1) how large and financially/emotionally important is the transaction; (2) how often is a transaction likely to occur and what other connections/interactions with the customer will take place between transactions: and (3) how easy is it for the customer to change vendors, services or products and how readily available are competitive offerings?

But, regardless of a given cycle's duration, there are similar cycles to be identified, tracked and managed in <u>every</u> business and properly managed, these cycles are the keys to closing the back door and keeping your customers for life.

CLOSE THE BACK DOOR – PART 2

I'm always surprised that even the smarter entrepreneurs, who understand how to segment their customers by "spend" and – within reason and usually discretely – treat them differently, fail to appreciate that simply approaching customers based on the dollars they contribute to your revenues is at best only taking into account a modest fraction of the whole story.

To really master the art and the science of customer retention, you've got to also understand where each customer is from time to time on the consumption cycle (as I described in the last post) and, equally importantly, you've got to determine what type of attachment the customer has to your business and the extent of the attachment that he or she has as well. And finally, you have to learn what viable alternatives and substitution capabilities the customer has and how compelling any available competitive offerings may be to each customer.

For the moment, I want to concentrate on the attachment issues because the conclusions you reach about these considerations will be the primary drivers of how you approach and treat each customer. Basically, you'll need to use different "strokes" (data, incentives and offers) for different folks if you want to succeed in holding on to the vast majority of your customer base. One size <u>never</u> fits all. And, the loyalty profiles of your customers will vary dramatically depending on the industry you're in and the specific kind of product or service that you are offering.

In the attachment universe, the first thing to determine is what type of connection is common within your industry and for your product or service. It's not as simple as you might think. And, if you do think this stuff is obvious or that you are already doing the right things simply because you "know" the answers to these kinds of questions (although you have to admit that you never really asked them or thought about them), then you're most likely in trouble already because anyone today who thinks that they have no "customer" issues or problems is just one step away from the cliff. The choice is always the same – innovate and improve your game or risk becoming irrelevant before you even realize it.

Step one is your industry/product. Soft drink and beer companies have it pretty easy. So do soaps, detergents, and deodorants. In fact, the most likely cause of a change in a beer drinker's preference is immediately following a divorce. Go figure that out. Probably not a lot of fond memories associated with your ex's brewski. But, in any case, in these industries you're looking at customers who have a clear emotional connection to the product and a reluctance to change or even try new products. They think they made a smart and conscious choice; they're sticking with it; and they're pretty good spenders as well. They're not going anywhere and you shouldn't allocate your scarce resources against this population because you always need to focus on changing the behavior of the "at-risk" customers – not necessarily stroking the ones who are already fat and happy. Call these guys the "HEART" group.

And, at the other end of the fun scale, in the life insurance business, you have an equally important group to ignore. This is another group that's going nowhere fast and maybe not until they die. I'd say that these people – by and large – apart from seeing the occasional FUD commercial on TV about your uninsured family ending up in the poorhouse and unable to bury you – don't even think about the product more than once a year; don't think there's any reason to change if and when they do; and aren't really even price-sensitive because who can figure out what any of this insurance stuff costs anyway. So, if the drinkers are emotional, these guys fall into the "just sit there" category. As long as you (or anyone else) don't disturb them, they're there for the duration. Same category includes your internet provider (notwithstanding a new bundle every day) and your credit card(s) company. It's just "too hard" to make a change that isn't precipitated by something. (By the way, this is not the same for car insurance decisions where there's so much ongoing and in-your-face advertising at all times that you're forced to consider apparent economic alternatives.) Call these folks the "BUTT" group.

The next and largest category (and the one you need to engage) can typically range very broadly across a lot of day-in and day-out necessity-driven products and services that we buy and consume almost every day – this can be our grocery shopping (but not personal hygiene items where we have an emotional connection as noted above); clothing for the kids; gas and maintenance for the car; etc. and here we're pretty engaged and VERY sensitive to and receptive to strokes. These are the folks who think a lot about their purchases (especially in these tough times) and they are regularly trying to evaluate, calculate and select the best deals. They are price/value/performance shoppers and they require a great deal of care and handling because of how quickly their loyalty and shopping habits can shift based on what you might regard as minor changes in price, packaging, bundling, etc. They need to be reassured and provided with continuing demonstrations that their choices and selections are the right ones. Call the guys the "BRAIN" group.

Take some time to figure out where you sit in this analysis and in the next chapter on closing the back door, I'll tell you what to do about keeping almost all of your customers on board for lif

CLOSE THE BACK DOOR – PART 3

When it comes to retaining your "BRAIN" oriented or analytical customers who represent the largest single portion of all of your customers in almost every circumstance, the process is straightforward and simple, but not easy to accomplish. You need to have a "conversation" with these people in order to address their concerns and provide them with the "strokes" necessary to convince them to stay.

But (a) you need to be very careful not to push or overstep their boundaries because they want to decide, not be convinced, in most cases; and (b) these kinds of "conversations" are almost always indirect and conducted passively rather than actively. It's not like sending someone a coupon in the mail or online or calling them up and telling them your dealership desperately needs used cars and how about trading in their car and getting a new one. And the job is much harder in industries where comparisons with alternatives are relatively easy and readily accessible and also where there aren't strong brand positions or attachments.

Keep in mind also that we're not talking here about unhappy customers (with or without a good reason) and we're not talking about customers whose changed conditions or circumstances have changed their requirements which in turn causes them to consider alternatives regardless of your efforts to anticipate and preempt such actions. Those cases require different approaches and typically aren't worth the incremental effort since the likelihood of a turn-around is small.

We're talking about generally smart, informed customers who try to act rationally and make the best and most cost-effective choices based on their view of the price/value equation which your products or services offer from time to time. And in most cases, they don't tell you if and/or when this process and the calculations are going on – they just do their thing. You've got to be your own best advocate and give them the tools, ammunition and ability to assess the situation and hopefully decide to stay.

Basically, there are 3 large buckets of benefits which you can manage and adjust to try to reach and convince these target customers. I call the buckets:

(1) Where's the Beef?

To borrow from Clay Christensen, the question here is how well does the product or service do its job? You need to determine how well you are doing relative to two metrics: the price/value equation (is it worth it?) and the cost of alternative solutions which may be readily available to your customers (where else can I find it?). Remember the old line that customers want ¼" holes, not ¼" drills. Whatever you can do to bolster and improve the customer's impressions in these two areas, you should do as quickly and as often as possible. The more benefits; the tighter connection; and the higher degree of "locking in" the customers and his or her peers to your service, the greater the likelihood that they will stay and not even consider switching.

(2) Where's the Heat?

The "heat" or, more accurately, the more friction that is built into your systems and processes, the more likely that there will be direct and negative customer reactions. Anything that takes too much time, requires repetition or seems to serve only your interests and not the customers' will be a problem going forward and a risk to your business. Remember that customers' buy for their reasons, not ours. Radio Shack has a pretty strong and flexible automatic return policy (even for cash purchases), but (for internal fraud prevention purposes), if you want a cash refund, they require that you supply them with your phone number. Turns out that for a lot of folks, this seems like gross overreaching and defeats the whole salutary basis of the general policy. The customer doesn't work for us.

Sometimes, businesses don't even really understand the "job" that the customer wants done and inadvertently make things harder or more expensive than necessary to meet the real requirements of both the customers and the businesses themselves. Customer loyalty punch cards are a well-intentioned retention device that (up until the advent of the new start-up Belly) was a literal pain-in-the-wallet (or purse) solution that was more often frustrating to customers instead of rewarding. How many half-punched cards can we jam in our wallet or forget to carry with us when we need them without bagging the whole bunch? Encouraging customers to consolidate their spending with you and return often is the holy grail, but only if the process is as painless as possible.

(3) Who's your Mama?

At the end of the day, everything in business and especially in successful selling is about relationships. The greater the connection and relationship that you can build with each and every one of these customers, the longer you'll keep them and the stronger they will be. Save me time or money or make me more productive and it's gonna take a very substantial and persuasive argument to make me walk away. And 9 times out of 10, price alone won't do it. The impression of "belonging"; being a special or top-tier customer; and/or receiving special perks and preferences are all methods that need to be continually expanded and built upon so that you constantly improve the connection to the customer.

No one sells a product anymore today – everything is a service in the sense that every sale should trigger a life-long customer maintenance program and strategy to maximize the long-term value of every customer and to help amortize their acquisition cost over the largest possible set of revenue streams and follow-on sales.

The best customers are those that "never come up for air" and then start to look elsewhere in the competitive marketplace because you've satisfied their past needs and their present requirements and you've anticipated their future desires.

THE ONE WHO CARES
THE MOST WINS

Remember when parents used to really care about their kids talking back to them or cursing? For a time, long after the weight and the sting went out of certain "swear" words and they were just words again in common use – albeit not universally, some kids (mostly younger brothers and sisters) still tried using them for effect and to rile up their folks, but it was pretty clear that no one actually cared that much. Sticks and stones, etc. Plus, and maybe most importantly, saying this kind of stuff and meaning it – even assuming that the kids knew what the words actually meant – were two dramatically different things. And their parents got that, refused to take the bait, and generally let a lot of "noise" just slide.

But their older brothers and sisters didn't waste any time in figuring out the most telling and effective new parental taunts to get under their folks' skins again and they deployed them so efficiently that even the grown-ups got with the program and adopted the new jargon almost overnight. And, somewhat amazingly, it was a single word that said it all for at least an entire generation.

And what was that word? It was "**whatever**" (shoulder shrug optional). In so many ways and so many circumstances and situations, "**whatever**" said it all and got the job done – smoothly and succinctly. And, what exactly does "**whatever**" really mean? It means "I don't care enough to care". So there!

It's one of those things that Aaron Sorkin only wishes that he could have added to the vernacular. For the moment, he'll have to settle for "ya think?" and a few other choice phrases that you can view <u>ad nausem</u> on the various YouTube *West Wing* or Sorkin compilations. And who's the very living embodiment of "**whatever**" every week on our TV screens? Of course, it's Dana Brody, the daughter from *Homeland*. If Carrie cares way too much about everything, Dana pretty much lets her Mom know every single episode that she doesn't much give a rat's ass about anything that her Mom cares about and she sure lets it show.

But why should any of this matter to you? We're pretty much in business after all – not entertainment, TV or the movies. But, as I've said before, no one sells a product any more – we're all in the service business now – where the key deliverable is the ability to create in the customer's mind the feeling of being sincerely cared for and cared about. Frankly, no one cares how much you know or how good you are at your job (except maybe if you're surgeons who apparently aren't required to have a personalities) - until they know how much you care about them. Caring costs a lot, but in the end, your people not caring is what kills businesses.

So the reason that the "**whatever**" phenomena should matter to you and your business is because the real message of "**whatever**" – which is an in-your-face, calculated, and painfully obvious indifference (however sincere or insincere it may be) - is a fact of life these days in too many places and, if you let it creep into your business and particularly into the attitudes of your people, you're screwed. Your customers will leave in droves. And they won't be back.

This is more critical than you think and something that gets overlooked too easily in the frenzy of rapid growth. I'm not talking about warm and fuzzy stuff – or Kumbaya crap – I'm talking about everyday execution of the fundamentals in your business. The truth is that, if as you grow, your people can easily get a little "tired" and think they have too much to do and that customers are a bother and too demanding and somewhat inconvenient, and when they start communicating that indifference to your customers, it's actually worse than you can imagine. It's like a slap in the face to the customers and they will pick up on it in a flash.

Why does it happen? First, it's not necessarily intentional and evil in many cases. Almost anything can get routine and repetitive and it's a short step from there to indifference. Second, passion isn't an infinite resource and it needs to be reinforced and replenished regularly. Third, today's younger employees are hard sells in a lot of ways. You need to keep in mind that at work they are generally more afraid of boredom than failure. And finally, anything that keeps growing and getting bigger always runs the risk of distancing your best people from the immediacy of the constant contact with your customers which is the very best feedback and reinforcement loop there is. Hearing the news – good and bad – from the horse's mouth is critical to keeping your people's heads in the game.

So, just like it's unsafe at night to speed so fast that you "overdrive your headlights" and can't see far enough ahead to safely stop in an emergency, a young company can outrun and outgrow its own energy and enthusiasm as it expands and burn out - not only lots of its loyal customers, but plenty of its best long-time employees as well. And when you do that, you find out that you've ended up with the <u>wrong</u> answer to the universal question: how big can we get before we get bad?

What can you do? You've got to spend the time and the resources to constantly reinforce the main message: that businesses exist because they have customers and taking care of your customers is ALWAYS Job Number One. Everything else can and should take a back seat to making sure that your customers know that you are looking out for them. And you've got to do it with a vengeance – with all your heart and all your energy. You don't get to fake it until you make it in today's super-savvy world. Second, the very best cure for employee boredom and indifference is challenge and curiosity. There is no cure for curiosity and your job is to make sure that your employees are always looking at new opportunities and new challenges. Finally, as always, focus. The smartest people I know care passionately about the few things in their life and in their business that really matter – the right things - and don't waste a minute or give a damn about the rest.

As you're trying to build your business and change the world, it's a good idea to remember that a different world can't be built by indifferent people.

TRICKED TRAFFIC ISN'T WORTH THE TROUBLE

An age-old question. If a tree falls in the forest, but there's no one there to hear it, does it make a sound? Who knows and who really cares? The better and more pressing question these days is: if the primary drivers for traffic to a website that you're paying money to advertise on are hacks, tricks and clever pet pix; what are the visitors who do show up (even assuming they are people and not tracking robots) really worth to you or anybody else?

I'd argue that they're not worth your time and certainly not worth any money you're paying for the very modest privilege of "entertaining" (in the loosest sense of the word) a bunch of morons with nothing better to do than to waste their time randomly clicking on just about anything. Instead of attracting people who might actually be interested in your products or services and also highly influential, you can end up spending money to attract mobs of easily-influenced people instead who probably couldn't explain how they go to the website if they were asked.

One of the things I always told restaurant owners about *Groupon* daily deals was that they were designed to attract "cheapies" to restaurants that were only looking for one-time deals instead of "foodies" who could become regular patrons and the true lifeblood of the business. And since I'm from Chicago and everyone's picking on *Groupon* these days, let me just say that we use it and that it makes sense for a lot of different kinds of businesses and situations IF you keep in mind 4 basic rules about when to do a daily-deals kind of deal:

1. The deal needs to drive new users and incremental revenue – not replace or cannibalize existing full margin revenues;

2. Your business can't be subject to capacity or size constraints which might result in the incremental traffic precluding access by and for existing customers and users;

3. The deal can't require you to spend or invest a great deal of upfront money with essentially sunk costs if the deal doesn't go; and

4. You can't put yourself in a position where taking on and delivering the deal gives you cash flow or other float problems.

But *Groupon* deals aside, there are still way too many companies "buying" into tonnage and volume (quantity rather than quality) and measuring their results by the wrong competitive metrics like "likes" and followers. As a result, the market continues to encourage young entrepreneurs to create (or basically make up) businesses which are all about buzz and bullshit rather than trying to build sustainable businesses which deliver real services and demonstrable results to clients and which have concrete economic rewards for those companies rather than cosmetic and superficial results that do nothing for any business's bottom line.

I keep seeing and hearing pitches and presentations predicated on prevarications, phony postings, and a pile of pictures that may be inexplicably popular, but have nothing really to do with anything and clearly nothing whatsoever to do with your products, services or business. As an example, I just sat through a highly-energized, but essentially empty, "presentation" about content and engagement which sadly, instead of being about ideas and approaches of substance, was all about scams and slick, but sleazy ploys to trick people into being traffic to sites for no good reason. A load of tactics and no real strategy or smarts. Or maybe they were really being just a little <u>too</u> smart for their own ultimate good. Because even if you're the biggest and fastest rat in the race, when the dust settles, you're still pretty much a rat.

ORIGINALITY IS REALLY OVERRATED

Although it shouldn't really come as a big surprise to anyone in sales, it turns out that selling someone something new and different is a lot harder to do than selling them more of the same or something that's just a little different and hopefully better. In fact, any salesman will tell you that the only thing harder to sell than something new is something people really don't want or need. That's when you know you're a real salesman. But, since most of us aren't super salesmen, we need to figure out other ways to overcome the simple fact that most people are just reluctant to try new things. Sometimes they're actually concerned or afraid, but mostly they're just inert – waiting for the world to happen to them – and not looking to try new things, spend extra money or take a chance on almost anything.

There are lots of reasons for this resistance, but the most basic reason is that we tend to like and to "go with" what we know. Tried and true solutions are safe, comfortable and relatively low risk. We're a conservative (not to say lazy) people and we're very happy to just get along and go along. This is probably a lot less true for entrepreneurs, but the sad fact of life is that the vast majority of the people buying whatever it is you're selling aren't gonna be entrepreneurs or risk-takers. And that's perfectly OK – it just means that you've got to learn to speak their language and put your selling proposition into a framework that they understand, appreciate and – most of all – are comfortable with. And it never hurts to make it your business to determine who the <u>real</u> buyers are and what the <u>real</u> drivers are for their decisions.

Let me give you a great example from my days of selling Xerox machines to law firms.

The first thing that you learn in dealing with law firms is that the senior partner who ultimately signs the checks rarely has anything to do with deciding the merits of the purchases he's paying for. He's too busy making money for the firm and it's not a good use of his time. This is also the case - 9 times out of 10 - with the owners of car dealerships. Generally, however, successful car dealers aren't spending their time making money for the firm; they're spending their money making time with hookers. But the idea's the same. And the minute something goes wrong, all these guys become screaming maniacs and want to fire the whole office. As a result, preserving the peace and quiet and not pissing off the boss becomes a consistent part of the purchase requirements.

The second thing you learn is that the other less senior partners in the law firm are a bunch of whinny, complaining assholes. I can say that because, for more than a decade, I was one. But here again, the real lesson is that life's too short to spend it listening to these bozos complain and, as a result, once again the decision set for law firm purchases has a lot to do with avoiding stress and strain and less and less to do with saving a few shekels. And, by the way, you wouldn't want to ask these nitpicking nutcases to participate in the purchase process under any circumstances if you ever wanted to get a decision made. Truthfully though they'd never let their fingerprints be found on any decision like this because it would theoretically keep them from second-guessing the actual decision-makers and from complaining about their conclusions.

So where does that leave us? With a simple rank order analysis of what you'd think the Xerox purchase decision set at a law firm consisted of and what the real criteria of the office manager (who's actually the buyer) turn out to be. In a survey of hundreds of professional office managers (including, but not exclusively, for law firms), the factors which consistently ranked highest had everything to do with keeping the machines up and operating successfully and almost nothing to do with costs. In order, they were:

1. RELIABILITY

2. COPY QUALITY

3. SERVICE

4. EASE OF USE

5. PRICE

And if you asked them honestly about their choices, they would initially offer you really nice clichés like: "when our copiers are working, our people are working", but the unspoken truth which eventually came out was always more like: "I want to keep my job" and "I don't want those assholes yelling at me." Saving money for the firm never entered into the equation.

The morale of the story is pretty simple. The most successful copier salesmen didn't pitch price, speed or performance – they focused on stability, security and the ever-golden "silence". They pointed their presentations directly at the pain points of the purchaser. And that won the day.

And the same approach and strategy works in almost any sales situation. You just need to remember 5 basic propositions:

1. Originality is overrated. Pioneers end up with arrows in their back - and not a whole lot more. Don't invent, innovate.

2. Novelty is a nuisance – it means expensive training; a new learning curve; and mistakes galore. Tried and true trumps all.

3. No one likes to cross the chasm – especially when they are first. Short, sure steps forward and a lot more of the same really sell.

4. Don't tell me how different your product or service is – tell me how easy and familiar and fail-safe it will be.

5. Analogies are better than apple pie. Show me anything I'm doing now and then tell me not how different things will be, but how much the same they will remain.

In the movie business, they call this process "high concept". You give me a snapshot that tells me all I need to know. Like using the latest slick and suave incarnation of Justin Timberlake to play the Frank Sinatra role in remakes of ANY classic Sinatra films. Says it all. I don't have to love the idea to understand exactly what you're telling me. Or having Tom Hanks play the Jimmy Stewart roles in anything except "*It's a Wonderful Life*". You get the picture.

Now think about what you're making and selling and figure out the same thing – what's the shortest pitch to get you on the path to a successful sale?

DOES IT MAKE SENSE TO "MAKE" ANYTHING ANYMORE?

A re we finally there? Should the last man out of tonight's late shift at the plant turn out the lights for good? Notwithstanding the success of *"Kinky Boots"* on Broadway, is the end of traditional manufacturing in sight? I'd say "yes" - albeit somewhat sadly.

There are at least six different drivers for the demise. And they aren't the obvious ones that you'd imagine – I'm not talking about outlandish labor costs, ridiculous OSHA regulations, or protestors more concerned about pollution and plant life than production - although we can certainly thank the bozos in Washington for making many things in the world of manufacturing much worse over the last two decades. My thoughts are a little more basic.

Here are my 6 D's:

(1) Dirt.

We lost the race for raw materials years ago as China and other more-foresighted countries scooped up vast quantities of all kinds of the mission-critical minerals, compounds and rare earths which are so essential to the production of the critical components of virtually everything cellular or digital in the world today. We don't have either the materials themselves or the right mindset any more. Maybe coal will stage a comeback. Here's hoping - not.

(2) Durability.

In a world of instant gratification and rampant disposability - where the packaging we negligently discard costs considerably more than the products we consume - who really cares about manufacturing durable goods and long-lasting products when we'll be sick of the stuff anyway once it's no longer shiny ? Shiny never lasts. In addition, new 3D printing technologies will permit and encourage the development of even more low-cost, immediate and discardable kinds of products – all in the "use once and toss" family and none of which is good for our production facilities, our population, or our planet.

(3) Demand.

Frankly, we'd rather not own anything these days. High maintenance costs, devastating depreciation of everything physical, rapid obsolescence driven by accelerating technologies, there's really no reason to buy anything for the long run. We're users and renters – not owners anymore. Zip cars are the "cars for people who don't want one" and that says a lot more about our lives today than merely about our transportation preferences.

(4) Desire.

Life today just isn't about things because the best things in life aren't things. It's not really that the nature of things ever changes; the fact is that our desire for certain things morphs over time and our appetites change as well. There's no such thing as pride of ownership either – it's not politically correct – because we all know that people are more important than things and bragging about your property and your possessions just isn't cool any more. We're seeing more and more that bigger isn't necessarily better. And we're also becoming much less materialistic. In the "*Mad Men*" world of not too long ago, they would say that 4 things defined a man: his home; his car; his wife; and his shoes. Just think about how little this formulation has to do with the way we see our lives today and you'll appreciate the massive changes coming down the pike.

(5) Demographics.

I wrote recently that kids don't care about cars, but the fact is that things are much worse for manufacturers than that. Apart from the prospect that today's kids may be the first generation that really isn't upwardly mobile relative to their parents, the fact is that - as soon as they reach the age where they would themselves determine and dictate durable goods purchases, they are finding that they don't have the dollars to do anything. Their folks stop buying them dolls, digital devices and indulging their every desire and they figure out pretty quickly thereafter that major purchases cost real money which they don't have and can't borrow. And instead of starting to save in order to eventually satisfy those deferred desires, they spend their time sucking down lattes from Starbucks. Everything today for Gen Yrs is about the experience and the adventure and the trip and not about things which are mainly a downer and a drag.

(6) Digital.

Digital is dictating everything and it's worth a whole column itself. But one thing's for sure – the kids today (and basically anyone with a brain) realizes that good ideas - regardless of their size - last much longer and are worth a great deal more than anything you can make with your hands and that - in this world of increasing connectivity - ideas can spread across the universe in an instant. Even more importantly, in these times of increasingly scarce resources, ideas (and digital goods) have an amazing and unique property – unlike even the best physical objects. You can share an idea with someone else (and/or everyone else) and then (unlike an apple or a Mac) – all of you have the shared idea – it's enhanced and expanded in its scope and its power - not diminished or lessened by sharing and broad distribution – and that's how we'll make our world will grow in the future – manufacturing new ideas – not new iPads.

WHAT I LEARNED FROM MY WAITRESS

I believe in life-long learning. I also believe that you can learn something of value from almost anyone. Everyone's an example - sometimes a good example - sometimes not - but always instructive. The key is to extract the wisdom from the wood chips and apply the lessons to your own work and/or life. It's easier said than done. For years, I've had a favorite waitress at my neighborhood deli named Brenda. I hate to wait for anything, but I'm happy to wait for a seat in her section because I think she actually improves my digestion. And she always shows me something. This week I learned three important things. It's always somewhat remarkable because very few people actually get tips from their waitress. So pay attention.

1. Repeat After Me.

I noticed that she has her own way of taking orders. She repeats everything that I say right back to me – word for word. And there's a curious comfort in that which is very reassuring. How many times have you had some smart-ass waiter stand there while you're reciting your very complicated choices and requirements and not write anything down or repeat a single thing? Did you really feel confident that your food was going to fill the bill or were you just a little anxious that maybe Wally the Waiter didn't really have the world's greatest memory and that your potatoes were coming with peppers whether you liked it or not? Not exactly the warm and fuzzy feeling that makes for return visits.

But the most important part of her process actually wasn't that she always got my order right. Her mimicry sent me a specific and powerful message. Not only was I being listened to; I was being heard. And I was being heard by someone who actually cared about me and about getting my order right. That emotional impression - that recurring result - the ineffable feeling of being "important" and cared for - is the absolute heart of great customer service. Getting the order right is basic execution. Getting the listening part of the process correct – basically adding communication to the conversation - was even more important. It's that old cliché – I don't really care how much you know until I know how much you care.

Way too often today we're distracted when we're supposed to be listening. We're texting or typing. We're multi-tasking or (not so discretely) checking our monitors for new email. And we're sending a very clear message to the person(s) talking to us. It says "I might seem to be listening, but you're not really being heard because my mind and my attention are obviously elsewhere" or it could be saying "I'm actually anywhere, but here in the moment and you don't really matter." Frankly, nothing could be worse for your people, your customers or your business.

If your customers don't think you're concerned about them or listening to them, they won't be customers for long. And it's even worse internally. If your people bring you problems or concerns and you seem too busy to listen or to be bothered, it won't take them too long to conclude that you don't care. They'll stop coming to you and, far more critically, they'll stop caring themselves. It's when your people stop bringing you their problems that you know you have a real problem.

So, if you're going to have a meeting - make it as short as possible - make sure it's necessary and not window dressing or make-work - and make sure it matters (so you aren't meeting for the sake of meeting). And then, if you're gonna do it - do it right. Be there 100%. Pay attention. Listen carefully. Take notes. Give them some feedback and a reaction. Make sure your people know they're being heard.

2.   Do What You Can Do.

My waitress doesn't own her restaurant and therefore she doesn't get to set the prices on the menu or the size of the portions. She doesn't determine the daily specials and she can't guarantee that they've got my favorite fruit on any given morning. Sometimes there are things simply beyond her control – like a new cook or busboy who just can't get things right. And shame on her for forgetting the surcharge for sharing. And - heaven forbid - she better not ignore the "no substitutions" rule which apparently is the Eleventh Commandment of the Bible of the restaurant business. So, given the many things that can get in the way of her delivering the kind of service and experience which makes a difference to her customers, she has developed her own simple strategy. She does what she can.

That may sound simplistic and somewhat random, but it's not that at all. This isn't some arbitrary process. It isn't a case of flouting the fat cats or trying to get away with something. The fact is that it's good for business to take care of your "friends" - the regulars - the special customers who represent the recurring foundation of the business. And that's exactly what she does and here's how she does it.

You say you don't want the green beans that come with your meat loaf. But the rules say "No Substitutes". Well, she doesn't substitute anything – she just piles on extra potatoes and lets you know it's a double portion. Not so good for the waist line, but great for making sure you know you're special. She can't change the rules, but she works her magic with the ladle. She works with what she has control over and she does what she can and it shows and – believe me - it matters. This is her own individual solution. When you incorporate this kind of flexibility and empowerment into your entire organization, you become Nordstrom's – the epitome of empowered employees and a great place to shop.

The trick that can make a difference in your own business is to figure out how to encourage initiative and how to give all of your people permission to make things special for your customers in their own personal way.

3. Don't Worry, Be Happy

If our jobs were fun every day, I think they'd eventually change the name and stop calling it "work". But at the end of the day, every job turns out to be a direct reflection of the amount of time, effort, commitment and passion you put into it. There are really no boring jobs; just people who are bored with their jobs because they lack the energy, attitude and imagination to make something great out of every day. The best bosses I know make it their business to find the pumped-up people in their places and make sure that their excitement, enthusiasm and energy is shared and communicated throughout the organization.

What I love about Brenda the waitress is that she absolutely refuses to let anyone be the "bad" in her day. On her worst day, she's a smile waiting to happen and you just can't knock her off her stride because she makes it her business to make your day in some little way. Her enthusiasm is absolutely authentic and completely contagious. There's no question that it's possible to take the joy out of any job. But you couldn't get her down if your life depended on it. This isn't just about being Peppy Pearl every day – it turns out to be communicating a different and far more important message.

It's about attitude and respect. It says that her job may not be rocket science or Earth-shatteringly important – but she takes great pride in how she does it and she puts herself entirely into the process. She expects you to appreciate that and to respect her effort and commitment to doing the best job of her job that she can do every day. And, unless you're completely unconscious, you do.

EVERY ROSE HAS ITS THORNS

I'm convinced that not only does every rose (think: customer, not garden) have its full complement of thorns, but that – in the case of start-ups - it seems to be the case that the prettier and larger the rose, the stickier and more challenging its thorns can be. And if there's one situation that's among the most difficult, it's the case of the 800-pound gorilla buyer who's an early and crucial customer (often representing a make-or-break deal for the whole business) and whose demands and requirements would drive a saint insane. If you're starting a business and you haven't seen this particular movie yet, trust me, it's just a matter of time.

Even though we all say that - in the final analysis – what start-ups need more than anything else is paying customers (and presumably the more and the bigger the better), the fact is that one or two big customers don't make a business and, worse yet, they can actually reduce your chances of success in the long run. It's critical to remember that too much dependence on one big customer can: (a) divert your attention from the real prize which is to diversify your business (and your risks) among a broad spectrum of customers of all sizes and shapes; (b) drive you nuts with customization and one-off development and configuration requests which can actually consume precious and scarce resources and end up making your base product offerings not viable or salable to the larger population of "regular" customers; and (c) put substantial and unwarranted downward pressure on your pricing which will reduce the critical early operating margins that are essential to any start-up's survival. You need healthy margins as early in your business as possible to give you some cushion and breathing room and to offset the mistakes and problems that you're sure to encounter.

How you negotiate with and respond to these "big dogs" can impact your fledgling business for years to come and, more specifically, the outcomes of these kinds of negotiations can be critical to: (a) your ability to fully and fairly price your products and services going forward ('cause you ain't gonna make it up on volume); (b) your ability to grow and expand your business according to your priorities and best interests;

and (c) most importantly of all, your ability to attract and secure additional strategic and sizable customers who will often be direct competitors of these initial customers.

This is a page I've ripped right out of the book of "be careful what you wish for" and plenty of people will be happy to tell you that big early buyers can be too much of a good thing for a young company in many different ways (staffing and scaling issues, financing and cash flow questions, quality delivery and control problems, etc.), but they don't go on to tell you what to do about it. And there actually are some good reasons for their reluctance to "talk turkey" apart from the fact that many of them are just "consultants" who are basically a bunch of blowhards talking a good game, but disappearing when it's time to actually roll up your sleeves and do something.

One real reason why a lot of the conversation and writing around these crucial issues are so painfully broad and general rather than specific and useful is because there are too many variables and diverse concerns for any one approach or set of answers to cover even the majority of the most typical cases. I understand this "one size doesn't fit all" situation as well as anyone and so my basic plan here is to give you some ideas and strategies for handling just one of the most important and recurring demands that large initial customers can make. It's one that I've found over and over again is likely to raise its ugly head sooner or later in almost every instance regardless of the industry, product/service offerings or other circumstances.

It's the demand for exclusivity and it's a killer. But it's a bullet you can dodge if you're prepared in advance with a series of reasonable explanations as to why it's actually not in that customer's best interests to insist on exclusivity. If you do this well enough, it may actually sound like a favor that you're doing for them rather than a product of the fear for your fleeting future that it's actually designed to mask. And keep in mind that this needs to be an ongoing topic of discussion and reinforced regularly with the customer because when you're dealing with these guys, the negotiations often just begin after the contracts are signed rather than coming to a happy conclusion with the stroke of a pen.

Since efficient and timely access to accurate and extensive information (especially personal and intent data about your customers and prospects) is going to be the major competitive weapon of the future in most competitive marketplaces, and since so many of my own businesses have been in these areas, my suggestions tend to reflect specific arguments that have consistently worked for me in the past in industries as diverse as automotive, insurance, hospitality and technology.

I assure you that these haven't exactly worked overnight and not without some interim concessions and "necessary evils" thrown in, but, in the long run, they will get the job done. Most of your customers will also put a major premium and considerable value and importance on the quality of the information and data that you are employing and providing and their perspective in this regard forms the foundation for several of the more compelling arguments.

So you might say: "I can't work exclusively with you because:

(A) it's important to both of us that the information, research, evaluations, prices, data, analysis, etc. (hereafter the "material") that we are relying upon for you and supplying to you be INDEPENDENT of your organization; and/or

(B) it's important to both of us that the "material" be OBJECTIVE and NEUTRAL and that the outcomes and results derived from the "material" are fair and unbiased in every respect; and/or

(C) it's important to both of us particularly as against third-parties (consumers, regulators, governments, etc.) that we quickly develop an INDUSTRY STANDARD which is agreed-to and accepted by all of the parties in the marketplace and which our company aspires to become; and/or

(D) it's important to both of us that we have enough customers and scale to permit us to make the necessary research and development INVESTMENTS which we could not undertake or afford on behalf of a single client or customer – regardless of its size; and/or

(E) it's important to both of us that we grow quickly enough and have a broad enough customer base that we can actually provide REDUCED COSTS of our products and services (but not artificially depressed prices) because we are able to realize the economies of scale and amortize our capital expenditures over the broadest customer base possible; and/or

(F) it's important to both of us in order to service your requirements on a national basis that we have other customers whose presence in certain parts of the country is larger than yours and whose commitments will justify GEOGRAPHIC EXPANSION into areas where your business alone would be insufficient to support our roll-out or operations.

Keep in mind that there's no simple formula for success or failure in these things. These approaches will help – some better than others – and some may not apply at all. Don't try to use every argument all at once – negotiations can often be wars of attrition and you want to always save a new argument or two for next time so that there will be a next time. But, if you work through each of them and try to determine for your own business (and on your own terms and in your own words) how similar ideas might help support your position, it's safe to say that you'll get a much better outcome than going in blind. If you know the pieces going in, you're much more likely to walk out with at least part of the pie.

Sometimes, by the way, it's clear that you just have to take what you can get now and hope that you can get what you want (and will ultimately need) down the road. If you wait too long or push too hard, you may find that you will just miss the whole deal. So try these arguments and see how well they work for you, but be careful not to be such a hard-ass that you end up throwing out the baby with the bathwater.

WILL YOU LOVE ME <u>MORE</u> TOMORROW THAN YESTERDAY?

In today's frantic, fast-forward environment of accelerated discovery of everything combined with the pressures of the constant quest for the newest "new" and for exponential excitement and stimulation on steroids, it's hard to know what a start-up should try to hang on to and make its own. We're in a time where the rate of abandonment is ten times faster than the rate of adoption for new mobile applications across every material age cohort. We're all great grazers these days, but we're harder and harder to corral for the duration. It seems clear that nothing is "the future" for very long these days and the cycle time between blips as well as the mean time between surprises (good and bad) keeps shrinking. In the world of 6 to 15 second videos, Andy Warhol's old 15 minutes of fame seems like an eternity and a tired remnant from another time.

Where everyone's trying to make the biggest splash, it's way too easy to lose sight of what really matters in building value for your business. You can easily lose the substance if you're spending all your time chasing shadows and shout-outs. You've got to set a steady course and a strong pace, but you can't get ahead of yourself – you want to move without undue haste, but without rest or interruption as well. I know that today – probably more than ever - immediate user engagement is certainly a critical component for a successful business because it's a race and no one is going to wait for you, but the truth is that, even in the near term and certainly in the long run, simply novelty, notoriety or even having the biggest, boldest launch in the history of man won't get the most critical job done. The trick is to live a lot longer than your launch. Even the best launches (think of Steve Jobs and *Apple* of old) are like forest fires or tornadoes – there's a lot of light, heat, sucking and blowing at the beginning and at the end, if you're not careful, you'll lose your business and/or your house.

There's no doubt that customer engagement is essential, but sustainable user/ customer retention (which doesn't need to be maintained constantly maintained by one-off efforts and/or repeated, massive and costly marketing salvos) is the whole ball game. Increasing retention isn't easy, but it's a lot easier to achieve when you understand the basic behavior drivers involved and then build your own program to support and optimize these types of connections and incentives for your users to return and remain.

The best and most successful players in this area are masters of what I call "manufactured addiction". It's the art of making sure that your users will love you even more tomorrow than they did yesterday. And all it takes to succeed is a basic understanding of human nature and a plan that capitalizes on some of our most basic emotions.

Here's the short list of the fundamental ideas and the emotional "drivers" that your engagement and retention plan should incorporate:

(1) We are basically lazy at heart. We'd rather have simple and stupid things done for us than do them ourselves. Especially boring and repetitive things. We'll happily exchange our loyalty for improvements in our productivity, savings of time and effort, or other actual dollar benefits. Everything today is a "deal" – we engage in constant calculations of the personal and typically immediate value of various proposed transactions – and – as often as not - we make these repeated determinations automatically and almost unconsciously.

(2) We hate to waste our time and we especially hate redundancy. It's like watching paint dry except that paint only has to dry once. How many times have you found yourself in situations where you are asked to supply (in one way or another) the same information again and again. I think that (other than making well people physically ill) requiring millions of us to repeatedly complete ridiculously redundant documents may be the most horrible injury that hospitals have regularly heaped upon the human race. Socially-engineered tools and underlying systems (like the omnipresent *Facebook Connect* button) which avoid the constant need for new site users to re-supply the same data over and over again and which have the additional bi-lateral benefit of saving programming costs and other work for the owners and operators of literally more than 10 million independent websites and services to date are extremely powerful connectors and hugely successful retention devices.

(3) We don't know when to quit. Once we have mentally "invested" our time and energy into any enterprise or activity, we are much less likely to abandon it. We believe for no good reason that even trivial actions over time have a cumulative value (although we couldn't quantify it or explain what it might

be) and that as a result of our steadfastness and continuity, we're sure to get lucky and be rewarded someday. In addition, we seem to always believe that our switching costs are much higher and more onerous than they actually are – especially in today's highly-portable and mobile world of the cloud. We're just suckers for the daunting power of the *status quo*; we are resistant to all unnecessary changes; and – as a result - we are virtually incapable of bestirring ourselves and choosing any less-than-overwhelmingly-compelling alternative to doing almost anything. And even the most useless, trivial and fleeting rewards (ranks, powers, badges, scores, etc.) make the choice to leave just that much harder.

(4) We don't want to disappoint our friends. The more "connected" we believe we are in any context to numbers of others (especially our friends, neighborhoods, families and peers), the less likely we are to cease an activity and the longer we will remain – even when the activity or venture has largely ceased to hold any personal interest for us or provide any real value to us. Misery loves company and we often underestimate the power of peer and other social pressures even among grown-ups. It's the contagious power of the crowd. And, for ourselves, there is a palpable (and demonstrably solipsistic) sense that - in "leaving" even the most useless environment, website or other fruitless activity – we are abandoning our "friends" and depriving them in some sense of the benefit of our continued presence. As if they really knew or cared.

(5) We all do much more from habit than from rational and conscious choice. The repeated use of and reliance upon any product or service tends to take on the attributes and associated behaviors of a habit and habits for humans are very hard to break and die hard. When habits are reinforced by peer pressure, collective action and other group dynamics, the "locked in" nature of the commitment becomes even more difficult to dislodge. We don't appreciate how "sneaky" and powerful habits can be because they begin as weak tendencies (which we think of as intentional preferences) and their power isn't readily apparent to us until they become so strong and controlling that we discover they are actually embedded and compulsive behaviors which are very hard to break. Make your product or service easy to use, readily accessible and friction-free and you'll own me.

(6) We all want to be leaders, not losers, and everyone today keeps score. This is why cab drivers who couldn't necessarily count to 10 can quote you precise opening night movie box office grosses for their favorite films. We're competitive – especially with our friends – and (at least on both coasts) in many cases, it's even more important that our friends lose (place lower

on any list you choose) than it is that we win. It's a little like the two guys running away from a hungry bear. You don't have to beat the bear – you just have to outrun the other guy. This means that, while leader boards have a certain definite appeal, peer-to-peer comparisons are far more compelling because – while you may not know the leaders – you always know want to know where you stand relative to your friends. I call this the "peer-spective" approach because although everything is relative, only things that are relevant to us as individuals will really compel or change our behavior. We're all status conscious and it turns out – pretty consistently – that while even money and other financial considerations will max out, there's no clear limit on the power of meaningful status-flavored achievements and rankings to drive increased and extended performance in both business and social contexts.

(7) We live in a "what have you done for me lately?" world. Just like Walmart and Costco religiously change their end-caps and in-store displays every week so that customers are always seeing something new, any site that doesn't feed the new, fresh content beast is doomed. Return visitors come with a set of progressively higher expectations – not only that the site will "know" them and simplify their progress – but that they will be offered new and extraordinary experiences and challenges or opportunities on each visit. Yesterday's miracle is today's table stakes and the ante is always being upped. There are two solutions to this problem. One is to hire more people and constantly obsess about the need to create clever new content. This is almost as bad as doing nothing and much more expensive. The second, and far smarter way to go, is to free-ride on obvious and available content that is being generated regularly and consistently by other providers. I'm not talking about stealing and I'm not talking about just copying super-popular content from elsewhere. I'm talking about simply setting down with a national events calendar and building a full year of piggy-backing your content currency strategy off of the constant and recurring flow of events, activities, anniversaries, holidays, films, etc. that beat a path to your door (as well as everyone else's) all year long. This seems so obvious that you would think it would form the foundation of virtually every site's programming and yet almost no one (except GOOGLE which does a new header every day) takes the few hours of creative thinking and organization that would make sure that they had a fresh, new, almost automatic stream of content ideas which the entire rest of the entertainment, news and media world were engaged in promoting for them. How much easier and cheaper could it be?

(8) And finally, we all want to drive the train. In their personal relations and leisure time, many young and active social media users want to have as much

impact and control as possible to make up for the frustration, helplessness and impotence they often feel at work. This sets up an interesting problem for many websites. If everything is too easy to accomplish, secure or achieve, the users lose interest; they aren't being challenged in any respect; and they don't value the results of their efforts. They want an active role in the process – they want to be the accelerating gas pedal which will drive the experience rather than the speedometer which only measures and displays the results. They want to see how their efforts and actions make a concrete difference in their status and/or their results. I suppose there are some people who would accept a fundamentally passive experience, but they aren't really the attractive and active users you looking for. As Yogi Berra used to say: "you can observe a lot by just watchin' ", but this isn't baseball. We want the people who make things happen – not the ones who watch what happened – or worse yet - the ones who wonder what happened. When your users are part of figuring something out and accomplishing even interim goals, they're going to be much more committed to the enterprise and to its success. The best and most compelling sites convert initial involvement into active engagement and then engagement into return and retention – all as a part of one seamless process. And, equally importantly, the most enticing sites are <u>fast</u>. Whether we realize it or not, every time we visit a site, in one way or another, we're expecting and hoping to learn something and the key to effective learning is the immediacy and accuracy of the feedback. We're not checking the calendar here – we're watching our watches because the cycle time for everything these days is in minutes, not months. Everything is in the moment and if you want me to come back, you've got to deliver the goods every time I visit.

IT'S ALWAYS TOO SOON
UNTIL IT'S TOO LATE

One of the hardest things to learn in successful selling is to leave well enough alone. The trick – once you actually do make a sale – is to shut up and leave. Don't keep talking; don't overstay your welcome; don't get greedy; and don't try to gild the lily. Get the goods and get out. But there are two basic tools in sales that are even harder to master – especially for young entrepreneurs.

First, you've got to learn how to directly ask for the order. But even more importantly, you've got to adopt the discipline; develop the thick skin; and practice the persistence that it takes to ask for the order <u>every</u> time you get the chance. Without embarrassment. Without hesitation. Without apologies. And without blaming it on someone else as in "my boss makes me do this." What exactly does this mean? It means actually remembering to ask for the sale every time the opportunity presents itself; making sure that you do it with a vengeance; and creating as many opportunities to do so as you can. Every time you try - you get better. Practice actually does make a difference. You want to always be closing the sale.

If you're apologetic or reluctant or only half-convinced yourself that the customer needs to act and act now to sign the dotted line, or if you're sitting back in the weeds waiting for people to call you, then you might just as well save your breath and shut your doors. You can't sell anything sitting on your ass. And – as with most things in life - saying certainly doesn't make it so - only doing makes a difference that matters. Knowing what you should do or talking it to death, on the one hand, and actually executing on the plan – quickly, confidently, and consistently - are too often worlds apart. Success really starts when you just start doing the heavy lifting of getting the job done.

As I look around these days, I see more and more instances where the people who should be focused on closing deals are spending their time and energy making excuses for their clients and customers and justifying their inaction and lack of concrete results. The economy sucks – so what? Someone is still selling things – just not your folks. The recovery is really slow. Big deal. People still need someone's products and services. It oughta be yours. "Understanding" your clients' issues and problems is a very nice theoretical approach (actually I think it mostly sounds better in the literature than it works in real life), and when it gets in the way of making a sale, it becomes a much bigger problem for your business and one that you need to promptly address and solve.

Salesmen who emphasize customer empathy and offer a collection of "good" excuses for missing sales aren't really doing much of anything for your bottom line. It may help them feel better about themselves and their poor performance, but it won't get you across the goal line. Nothing happens without salespeople who <u>want</u> to sell your product. My best-ever sales manager had a simple (and admittedly crass) analysis which has always stuck with me. His view of the sales world all came down to a single idea: "somebody's gotta sell this shit". Feeling sorry for your customers doesn't really get anything done. You've got to nip this attitude in the bud and get your people back out there on the street selling. If they're not in the game, you can bet that someone else will be taking up the slack and making the sales. I hear these sad stories about missed chances & lousy excuses from companies every day.

One of the worst excuses of all is being told by the customer that the timing just isn't or wasn't right. You'll learn soon enough that it's always too early until it's too late. And nothing's a worse feeling than dropping the ball with a customer who keeps putting you off and off and then - when you finally do get around to calling again, they tell you that you're too late because they went with someone else. The longer I'm in business the more I realize that there's never a perfect time for the customer to buy because most of them would just as soon not buy if they don't have to - so it's the salesmen's job to control the clients' calendars; to always be in their faces; and to be there whenever the customers <u>are</u> ready to buy. It's all about "at-bats" and always asking for the order. Lots of important things are lost for lack of asking.

And here's an interesting fact. As brash, impolite and aggressive as most entrepreneurs appear, the fact is that they're no better (or more capable) than anyone else when it comes to this crucial skill. I don't think society in general has gotten a lot more gracious and polite lately (in fact I'd say it was exactly the opposite), but for some reason, young people today are reluctant to push and/or to appear to be pushy. Some otherwise tough and smart entrepreneurs I know would rather die than die of embarrassment. They don't think it's cool to let people see you sweat. They don't understand that it's a good thing – not a bad one – to show everyone exactly how much you want something and what you're willing to do to get it. Sometimes

I even think that – in their hearts and heads - they themselves doubt their products and services and this also makes it hard for them to throw themselves into the game full-force with body and soul. That tired old joke about sales has more than a kernel of truth. They used to say that the main difference between a car salesman and a computer salesman was that the car salesman knew he was lying. Maybe a little self-doubt also comes with every new digital business and maybe that's not a bad thing.

But, as I've talked to a bunch of these guys and girls, the real issue turns out to be simpler and – by the way – easier to resolve. Entrepreneurs aren't used to being told "no" and they don't like it. So they avoid it by not putting themselves on the firing line often enough and it slows down their businesses and their growth. It also sets a lousy example for the rest of the sales team. But I've got a simple mantra that can save the day.

All you need to do is train everyone in your business (including yourself) to repeat this phrase a couple of times a day – especially in the selling season – and it'll be much more helpful than all your pep talks, sticks and stones, sugary sweets and other threats and incentives combined. What's the phrase that I use to keep bouncing back up and taking the next step and the next shot and asking for the sale every day?

I say to myself and my team: "it's only a "no" for now". And, you know what, almost every "no" is exactly that – it's a "no" until it's a "yes" and it'll only be a "yes" if you keep asking.

BRAGGING RIGHTS ARE
THE NEW CURRENCY

Having just heard the Winklevii twins try to "explain" to a very skeptical Dealbook audience the rationale for their Bitcoin investment and what an exciting new form of currency it has become (nothing less than "Gold 2.0" so they say), I still had trouble figuring out exactly how Bitcoins were likely to change the financial instruments and payments world as we know it. But maybe that's just me.

Bitcoins are definitely a fast, fluid, flexible and "free" solution for effecting money transfers and those attributes are certainly among the most compelling components of any new and demonstrably disruptive technology. But considering the Ozian aspects of its mysterious founder, the apocryphal stories of its formation, and the vagaries of its current administration as well as the utter lack of transparency regarding many of the mechanical functions which allegedly make it work so smoothly, it's just hard to have a great deal of confidence in the whole thing.

So, for my two cents (no pun intended), as far as new "currencies" go, I'd rather bet on the best/worst tendencies and reliably consistent behaviors of ordinary people. One thing I know for sure is that we all revere status and that we all love to keep score and - most of all – that we love to compete with each other and especially with our friends and family. In fact, in many cases, just winning isn't really enough, it's just as important to know that your friends lost.

So I'm staking my claim on "status" in all its forms and flavors as the next great "currency" and, more importantly, as the most cost-effective and accessible influencer of changes in consumer behavior which is available to smart businesses of every size. Traditional forms of advertising are antiquated and virtually invisible – broad-scale, brute force marketing clearly costs too much and returns too little – but status abides.

And now is the time for you to learn how to incorporate these new behavior drivers into your relationships with your customers and prospects.

The fact is that we always knew that status mattered. But it's only with the comprehensive hyper-personalization of the web (thanks principally to *Facebook*) that these days we actually have to be whom we are because the days of Internet anonymity are long gone. And, as a result, it's become possible for any business to: (1) confer upon and award status to others (particularly its customers); (2) to reliably create, measure and track status, achievements, accomplishments, etc. on a massive scale; and (3) to broadly distribute and publish the results in real time to audiences – large and small – that matter to each and every one of us.

Lists of all kinds, leader boards, badges, rankings, etc. are some of the most obvious incarnations of the status tracking/measurement syndrome that's accelerating and being supercharged by social media. And these trends aren't limited to consumer forums – they're impacting and sweeping through the business environment as well. One of the earliest manifestations of this kind of behavior was aggregating "friends", "likes" and "followers" before we all came to appreciate that having too many friends wasn't exactly a good thing. At the same time, these early aggregations were generally enabled by a set of activities that consumers could directly manage and partially influence – if you spent the time, you could up your game and change your position. But today, that's much less true especially when you compare the old systems to today's tools like *Klout* and *Kred* which are primarily beyond the control of individuals.

I realize that *Kred* has certain self-reporting activities ("uploadable moments") that give its participants some sway over their individual rankings and ratings, but essentially these new measurement systems profess to be aggressively independent and objective even while they entice and encourage us to engage in activities which they claim to be influential in their calculation and evaluation processes.

And, by the millions these days, people are taking the bait and changing their behavior in the (most likely vain) hope that their actions will improve their stature and standings within these artificial (and largely irrelevant) hierarchies. I say "largely" irrelevant because – the fact pretty much is – that without a fairly robust and demonstrable *Klout* score these days – you can essentially forget about even getting an interview with a top tier advertising agency, PR firm or social media team.

But what does all this have to do with you and your business? Simply this. If you want to keep your customers and, in fact, deepen and extend your connection and relationship with them, you need to understand how these new notions of shared notoriety and the concept of manufactured addictions (where we repeatedly engage in activities for no real economic benefit or actual purpose other than improving our rankings or status on some utterly arbitrary listing or leader board) can be used by you to build better and more beneficial bridges to your customers which will increase their commitment and loyalty to your products and services.

There are basically 3 simple elements to the status equation which almost any business can create and implement (at little or no cost) and – in each instance – your job is to create the levels, tiers and plateaus (almost exactly as if you were building a typical computer game for your customers to play) which will help you generate the kind of quasi-competitive environment that triggers and spurs on this kind of compulsive/obsessive behavior and builds Power Users. Power Users who quickly become – not simply your most lucrative customers – but – even more importantly – your strongest, most authentic, and most aggressive advocates and promoters.

Here's a basic outline of what you need to think about and construct in the context of your business:

(1) Provide Increased Recognition for your Power Users

You need to develop a simple system to provide, document and publish the increased status and recognition which you are affording your most important customers. There are several companies already in this space who provide various programs with levels, award schemes, badges, etc. that can be easily adapted to your requirements. Just make sure that you take the time to personalize the offerings so that they don't just seem like the latest and greatest canned incentive program that some consultant sold you.

(2) Provide Expanded Access for the Power Users

As every restaurant, night club, airline and sports team learned long ago, there's always a "best" seat in the house and there are people who will do whatever it takes and stop at nothing to be granted access to those rarefied levels and locations. In the purest business context, this can range from special service lines, extended hours or credit considerations, concierges, accelerated processing or transport programs, etc. Here again, the incremental resources required to deliver these kinds of programs are trivial compared to the long term lifetime value of retaining these high-end and often hyper-active customers.

(3) Promote "Ownership" by letting Power Users Actually Influence the Business (or at least let them "think" that they are)

To a very real extent, the smartest companies today are designing programs and incentives which basically "hire" their own customers to work for them and encourage them to do significant amounts of work in the name of influence and ownership. Insurance companies are increasingly creating more self-service options for their customers and positioning these things as conveniences and tine-savers for their customers rather than cost savers for the companies which, of course, they are as well. Obviously, Wikipedia's 70,000 "editors" believe (and rightly so) that they are influencing the end product on a daily basis. And they will continue to do so without any thought of compensation so long as their efforts are acknowledged and so long as they don't feel that anyone is making a buck off of their hard work and good will. Users groups have been around for quite some time, but the difference is the immediacy with which, and the concrete ways in which, the influence of Power Users is implemented by these companies in virtually real time.

Frankly, this whole approach is just today's rife of the old Tom Sawyer fence painting scam. As Tom said to Ben: "Does a boy get a chance to whitewash a fence every day?" And a bit later, Ben asked Tom: "Say, Tom, let me whitewash a little." And the rest, as they say, is literature. Some things never change.

BUILD A SOLID SMART-UP, NOT A SKINNY (LEAN) START-UP

One of the great TV ads of all time featured a crotchety old Chicago woman (Clara Peller) whose plaintive 3-word inquiry ("Where's the Beef?") became a national catch phrase and a huge advertising home run in terms of brand awareness and sales for Wendy's restaurant chain. Every comedian, late-night television host, news commentator and politician seized on the expression and couldn't use it enough.

For at least an entire year after the commercial first aired, it became a very succinct way to challenge the substance of almost anything or anyone – even politicians like Gary Hart. It was a socially-acceptable form of 80's shorthand and a speedy substitute for those who formerly referenced the ancient (1837) and time-honored Hans Christian Andersen tale of the child who noted that *The Emperor's New Clothes* were notably absent.

And – amazingly enough – this lightning-fast phrase craze swept the country in 1984 – long before social media made it possible for the most trivial comment by a second-rate celebrity to become a worldwide "triumph" or "travesty" overnight. But today, among too many young startups, the latest and greatest craze – with roughly the same caloric count and value - is "lean" everything.

I find myself thinking fondly of Clara's pronouncement whenever I have to sit through another bogus business review session where someone with the bare bones of an idea is trying to convince a group of otherwise intelligent investors that there's a real business opportunity buried beneath all the bullshit and that (a) all of the shortcomings of the story being spun and (b) all the gaps in the gospel aren't actually problems at all. They're not bugs, oversights or misses; they're the intentional result of trying to be "lean" and trying to launch "something" (not to say "anything") to get the ball rolling.

I'm not sure when it got to be OK to try to do the least work possible in developing anything that you were seriously trying to do well, but maybe I missed a memo or two. And, as a result, when I hear these pitches and have people telling me that it's the minimum viable product, not the meat of the matter, that actually counts; I remember that Clara knew better and that this entire lean startup movement not only misleads and misdirects people into building mediocre products and potential services, it's also much more of a curse that ails us than any kind of a new cure.

We're encouraging an entire new generation of young entrepreneurs to rush things out to prospective customers; to throw a bunch of stuff against the wall; and to see what sticks. In the old days, people thought this might be a good way to test to see if the spaghetti was <u>al dente</u>, but it actually wasn't. Pasta that sticks to the wall is most likely overcooked and too gummy to taste good.

Like so many other things in life, there's no simple shortcut or quick way to do these things right. It takes time and craft and patience to build things that will matter and last. "Quick and dirty and out the door" sucks as a strategy for successful startups. Maybe you can never be too thin or too rich, but a startup can clearly be too "lean". The ultimate goal isn't to build skinny startups – it's to build smart ones.

I understand that it would be naïve to delay your launch until you thought you had every single detail exactly right and that, by waiting, you'd ended up building the completely perfect product or service. We know that, over and over again, even the experts can completely overlook glaring interface flaws or other obvious omissions that the simplest novice user will see right off the bat. And it's equally arrogant to assume that you can't learn a single thing from the marketplace or your users. But that's just a different problem.

As I see it, there's a basic flaw in the common understanding of the "lean startup" concept and then there are 3 main problems with the way most young entrepreneurs are trying to adopt and implement the methodology.

The Basic Flaw

Even the best MVP ("Minimum Viable Product") won't succeed without an MVA. An MVA is a Minimum Viable Audience (that's my simple shorthand for a bunch of potential buyers). Long before you start creating your product, crafting your code, and designing your UI; you need to find out if anyone gives a damn about your idea and your proposed solution. This isn't easy work. You have to actually get off your butt and get out into the field and find and talk to actual people – not your co-founders or your folks – about what you're hoping to do.

You have to find actual problems that are generating real pain for a large number of people. You have to determine whether those people recognize the problem, appreciate the pain, are willing to admit that they have the problem, and are willing to pay for a solution. Then you might have a fighting chance to define and build a viable solution.

And you have to also recognize that: (a) there's an infinite demand for the unavailable (anyone can say they'll buy something that you don't have for sale); and (b) the easiest way for a buyer to get you to leave them alone is to say "Yes" and "Come see me when your product is ready" and then show you the door.

The 3 Key Problems

They Won't Care

If you haven't done your homework first and identified the right pain points and the right target customers, you might as well take a hike because no one wants the cure for no known disease; no one is going to invest in solutions in search of problems; and you'll end up building and wasting a lot of time on the greatest software never sold. The way you start the process determines where you end up and these businesses are hard enough even for the people who do all the proper research, preparation and planning. A goal without a plan is just a daydream on someone else's dime.

They Won't Suffer

The idea that you can dump some partially-baked solution on your first prospects and that they will help you figure things out is another pipe dream. Trying to make your first users into your last beta testers is a stupid waste of everyone's time today because smart users want simple solutions that work right out of the box, not more problems. And it doesn't really matter what the problems are – implementation, training, support, stability, or security – they're all just more noise and aggravation that busy people don't need. We are very quick to try and even adopt things that work for us, but we're even quicker (by a multiple) to dump the stuff that doesn't. And while there is an obvious trade-off between the degree of the customer's pain and the customer's otherwise heightened expectations, in the end, no solution that simply swaps one set of problems for another is going to get out of the gate.

They Won't Wait

As the Heads & Shoulders people always say, you don't get a second chance today to make a first impression. Customers won't (and don't) wait for you to figure things out and – for sure – if your first attempt falls flat, you can bet that they won't let you come back. We hear too often about products that aren't released, but simply escape and others that aren't ready, but run out of time and race into the market. It's ridiculously easy to burn your bridges and impossibly hard to rebuild them when there are fast followers and copycats galore standing in your wake and watching your mistakes. Customers don't want stories or excuses; they want workable solutions.

The Right Way

There is a right way to do this and it's pretty simple. Do your homework and find an important unmet market need. Recruit the right early users who are invested (by virtue of their own desires) in your success. Build your MVP to their specifications and with their input and buy-in. And then prepare to enter the perpetual iteration loop.

Launch, Measure, Modify, Re-Launch and Repeat the Process <u>ad nauseam</u>.

Successful solutions today are all the same – moments of mad creativity followed by months of maddening maintenance. Continually raising the bar and improving your offerings is the only way to stay in the game.

SELF-SERVICE, SO WHAT AND DOWNRIGHT SCARY STUFF

Self-service business solutions are all the rage these days and that's good news in many cases. These kinds of programs can save us all a great deal of time if they're implemented properly and, frankly, in some cases – like ATMs – there's little question left today that we actually prefer the machine solutions to dealing with bored and indifferent tellers. But when self-service is poorly done, in big box stores for example, it can feel like you're wandering in the desert for days without ever seeing a helpful human being. And, as often as not, when you finally do come across a living, breathing person, it's generally not their department or they have no clue as to how to help you.

It's always struck me as very sad that so many of these large organizations with hundreds or thousands of front-line, customer-facing employees don't seem to understand that it's not simply about the rote training of their people; it's about building and reinforcing their team's self-esteem. If you can make their jobs "important" (whatever they are) and make them feel good about what they are doing every day (however seemingly mundane it may be), the people will get their jobs done and done well regardless of how many hours of lectures and useless training they have had to endure. Pride is just as contagious as Ebola and it shows.

And when big companies push the acceptance envelope too quickly or too aggressively, even in apparently modest ways where they are basically trying to save a few bucks, they can end up shooting themselves in both feet. A recent example from one of the nation's biggest banks is very instructive. To save money, they stopped sending deposit envelopes which had previously been printed with the return postage pre-paid. I guess they figured that, if their customers were mailing in a deposit, they could afford a stamp. Not the worst thing in the world, but chintzy nonetheless.

But I stopped by one of the bank's many branches a few weeks ago when I had used up my last envelope and asked for a few of those new "pay your own postage" mail deposit envelopes for future deposits. Amazingly, they told me that the branches aren't being given any envelopes to give out to customers for mail deposits. And, if you can believe this, when I asked them what the current address was for the mail deposits, they had to spend 5 minutes looking it up and they wrote it on a piece of scratch paper for me. I guess now you need to provide your own envelopes and your own postage. Seems like the beginning of the end of mail deposits or maybe they just don't care about the customers' needs any more. In any case, I'm not banking there anymore. Would you?

But I'm not really that concerned about crappy traditional self-service which I would call abuses and poor uses of the "Help Yourself" model. I'm more interested in where we're heading with the new technology-based approaches that shift a lot of the burden of interaction, authentication and other effort to the consumer. These programs might better be described as the new "Help Me Help You" model. And here too, as with most of these things, success or sucking is in the details and in the execution because - when it comes to service, everything matters.

It's also critical to understand the ever-changing boundaries of the typical consumer's acceptance of these increasingly intelligent (and somewhat invasive) automated interactions which are being driven by the adoption of new in-store technologies. These solutions are predicated on our increased mobility and connectivity and also depend and incorporate the staggering amounts of real-time data which our devices can now provide to interested and activated merchants.

Here are just five examples of what you can expect to see in the retail area alone:

(1) In-store displays that send texts and/or talk to you as you pass by them;

(2) Systems that track what you've purchased and suggest what you may have forgotten;

(3) Dressing rooms that read RFID tags on your selections and suggest alternative choices;

(4) Phone apps that make cosmetic recommendations based on analyzing your selfie; and

(5) Systems that project digitized versions of clothing or other products onto your body

Ask yourself just how creeped out you would be as each of these systems becomes more and more personal and personalized. And yet, realistically, as long as these exchanges are designed to provide real value on both sides of the deal – saving us time or money or helping us make better and smarter choices, I think that we've just seen the beginning of this trend and we will see expanding variations of it in every business very soon – including yours.

I wrote recently that it was important in trying to keep your own business on the leading edge of what was happening with emerging new technologies and other potentially disruptive changes for you to invest the time and make the effort to keep an eye on both the players and leaders in your own industry and also the smart and aggressive companies in adjacent spaces and market sectors where innovations that are transferable and readily-applicable to your own company's offerings and ways of doing business may be taking place. I called this process "lateral learning". (See:http://www.inc.com/howard-tullman/when-to-steal-from-other-founders.html)

I noted there that - as often as not - the observations that really paid off were those about companies which were testing for and continuing to politely push the acceptable limits of consumer behaviors and which were basically asking exactly what it was fair or reasonable these days to expect consumers (and especially your regular customers) to do as their part in the day-to-day transactions that make up our businesses. These companies are doing all of us a great service because, frankly, if these questions were not being asked and the responses acted upon; we'd still be doing a whole bunch of things in the old-fashioned and inefficient ways that worked for us in the past. Change doesn't happen on its own and someone needs to keep raising the bar and asking "why not" a lot.

But, if you want your own business to succeed, you really can't leave all the heavy lifting to the other guys and keep riding on their coat tails. The problem with the "After You Alphonse" strategy (playing it slow and safe and letting the other guys go first) is that, by the time you finally wake up and smell the coffee, they're over the next hill and miles ahead of you. And, the fact is that you're the ones who are supposed to know your markets, your customers and even your competition the best and so you're really the most likely candidates to figure out where things are headed in your industry, how to apply these new tools to your business, and just how far to go before you've gone too far.

NO MORE NAVEL GAZING

As the year draws to a close, and we all get a little break from our day-to-day activities (and from the regular crises and fire drills that accompany them), it's a good chance to find some time to catch your breath and spend a few hours just thinking – and not doing anything else, but thinking – about the year ahead and where you want to take your business.

I'm not talking about some foolish New Year's resolutions (like Zuck's optimistic, but stillborn, daily "thank you" plan) or your desire to definitely get in great shape this coming year or to be a much better person in 2015. I'm talking about thinking strategically about how you can make the next 12 months a lot more valuable and productive for your company.

This isn't about some make-work exercise, crystal ball predictions, or chart drawing contests – it's much more basic than that. It's not about making roadmaps – it's about your mindset. It's about you and you alone taking a moment to take stock of things and to ask yourself some very basic questions. There's plenty of time for group activities and facilitated/moderated conversations (whatever you might think those are worth) and/or sharing your wisdom with the team. But, first and foremost, you've got to make sure that you've got your own head on straight and fully back in the game.

None of us does enough of this simple exercise these days (we've all got plenty of explanations and excuses for why this is) and, as a result, too many businesses lose sight of the main chance, the critical things they need to be doing, and the most important questions they should be asking. Questions like: why did I get into this business in the first place? Am I doing any good and/or making any difference that matters? Does anyone outside of my friends, family, investors and employees care about what we're trying doing?

And while you're at it, I wouldn't waste much time reflecting on the past 12 months since: (a) there's nothing left that you can practically do about them; (b) you oughta already know what you did right and wrong since you lived through it and hopefully learned a lot from the experience; and (c) fretting over mistakes and missed opportunities doesn't really move anything forward. You want to build your future on strength and resolve and not on regrets and "shoulda, woulda, couldas".

But those are not even the main reasons why it's not effective to spend a lot of time looking backwards. Looking in the rear mirror is distracting and a great way to run off the road if you're not careful or to smack into something big and ugly that would have been a piece of cake to easily avoid if you had been paying a little attention to the outside world and, even more importantly, to what your customers are doing and saying about their own pressing needs and their current desires. Customer expectations are progressive. If you're not on top of them, you'll be at the bottom of their list of choices soon enough.

And the most important reason that you don't want to get all wrapped up in reliving and analyzing the past is that it's almost always an invitation to largely look inward. To spend your time navel gazing, making excuses, and bemoaning the bad breaks. It's mainly about you and your issues. And that's not where you need to be focusing your energy, your research, or your efforts as you try to get the business set for the New Year.

You need to get out and find out what's going on now outside the four walls of your business because that's where your future will be found and fixed or frittered away. We can surely learn from the past and we react every day to the present, but we can leverage and change the future. But that kind of change won't happen by itself. You've got to be asking the right people the right questions. And, right now, that's your most pressing job as a leader.

And here's a flash: you will never get straighter or more useful answers to your questions than the ones you get directly from your customers. The truth – with all its wonders and warts – comes from the consumers and the users of your products and services. They don't have any other agendas (apart from always wanting a lot more for a lot less) and they're the real reason you got into this startup mess in the first place so pleasing them and addressing their notions, ideas, and needs seems like the obvious thing to do. But it doesn't happen if you don't do it.

And here's some more breaking news: you might just discover (when you take the time to think, to look, and to ask) that there's a bigger and better opportunity right under your nose which you've been practically tripping over for months or years without ever noticing. One of our 1871 startups (We Deliver) thought they were in the delivery business for small merchants until they discovered that what those many businesses really needed was a mobile ordering app for their products and services which they couldn't afford to build for themselves. Even more importantly, when you roll up hundreds of those businesses into a one-stop, mobile ordering app that consumers quickly learn about from all the individual merchants – you basically create a destination platform (with critical mass) that also makes life a lot easier and more efficient for thousands of shoppers who can now aggregate and bundle their purchases from multiple sellers into a single transaction. And, by the way, all those additional products don't end up delivering themselves so the new platform approach also drove the basic business to new heights as well.

If you want to take the plunge, here are a few of the main questions to ask yourself. It's a pretty simple process, but, as you'll see, the results can be game-changing.

(1) What's the problem you initially set out to solve?

(2) Are you trying to solve the same problem today or doing something different?

(3) Is the problem still important to your customers and worth paying you to solve?

(4) Are there cheaper, quicker or easier solutions to the problems offered by others?

(5) Are there new, more important or different problems to be solved?

You'll notice that all these questions – in the first instance - address the customers' problem(s) and not your products or solutions. This isn't just a question of semantics. If you don't understand the pressing problems of your customers, you have no chance at all of building a successful product or service to solve them. You can keep building the greatest software never sold or the cure for no known disease, but you won't be building a business that will be here at the end of next year.

A SHORT TALE
ABOUT THE LONG TAIL

If you haven't been in a *Best Buy* store lately, you'll be surprised to find that – almost on a weekly basis – the Blue Ray/DVD department just seems to be shrinking right before your eyes. My guess is that - among all the big retailers - it's now a flat-out race to the bottom (and to the mid-aisle disk dumping bins) between the BD/DVD guys and the CD department heads whose in-store footprints are also approaching Lilliputian dimensions (not just at BBY, but in every other consumer electronics retailer as well) although the space share shift in the audio department seems to be slightly offset (or disguised) by the huge growth and substantial variety of new offerings in the headphones department. Thank God for *Beats*.

I think that *Best Buy*'s management is basically giving it up – waving the white flag - and just conceding that they're fighting a losing battle on too many fronts to continue the war. But they may be missing the boat because they're playing 100% defense (cost-cutting) instead of trying to get ahead of the curve and repositioning themselves to serve the <u>new</u> needs of their customers before their few remaining customers abandon them entirely. This isn't anything new in the category of Business Management 101 – the demands of customers are always changing and you either change with (or ideally ahead of) them or your customers go somewhere else. What has changed is the speed of the changes going on and how quickly you need to anticipate and then react to those changes in behaviors, attitudes and demands.

Here's what we know for sure today. Companies that have effective online <u>and</u> offline channels consistently and significantly outperform their competitors who are still using only a single channel – typically bricks and mortar. It's all about the interplay between the channels and about the mix of offerings in each and, most importantly, it's about the need to continually innovate and add new functionality, products, services and solutions to <u>both</u> channels rather than starving one and trying to double down on the other. Honestly, I think that the big box retailers bought into the inevitability arguments which were constantly being promoted by Amazon's press and PR blitzkrieg a little too soon and much too completely. As a result, now that the boat has pretty much sailed, I think we'll see that 2015 will be known hereafter as the year in consumer retail when the "tale of the long tail" really came true, but only because the major retailers helped stage their own funerals instead of fighting back.

And, as convincing as the long tail arguments seemed to be on the surface, it's turning out that the infinite inventory and instant availability attributes of the long tail were only part of the causes of the retailers' ongoing difficulties. These superficial factors masked - to a certain extent - another major contributing behavior. The hidden problem was that these freaked-out retailers are killing themselves slowly. They were trying to catch a knife and each concession that they made to reduce their in-store inventory exposure and their overall physical merchandise offerings turned out to make the overall situation even worse because – from the standpoint of even the most willing consumer – this process quickly became a self-fulfilling prophecy.

No one wants to waste a trip to the store once they're convinced that what they want won't be there anyway. This is the old *Blockbuster* paradox coming back to life – *Blockbuster* always had loads of empty display boxes for all the popular films and plenty of old product, but none of that week's hottest hits in stock. In other words, they had everything you didn't want and nothing you needed. And, what is also very clear today is that, while we're not watching any fewer movies or TV shows or listening to any less music (or – in fairness to my good friend Don Katz – consuming less "audible" content including music), we are increasingly accessing and absorbing whatever the desired content may be in virtually every manner except sitting in one place and "playing" a physical object on a fixed and immobile device.

So the critical underlying issue isn't decreased demand. I think that it has a lot more to do with portability. The rise of mobile computing and the ubiquity of constant connectivity has definitely put extra pressure on the old delivery systems and technologies and the big box retailers haven't done any more to address this transition than the booksellers. In a world where everything wants to be streamed, *Best Buy* needs to think of their stores as digital gas stations and provide fast, cheap and exclusive fill-ups on new music for their customers on the spot – in the store and online, too. The music is the real message, not the medium of delivery. We don't need shiny disks to share our sounds any more. *Best Buy* should stick to selling fans and fridges which won't be going digital any time soon. Phones and headphones will probably sustain them for a while because these objects (of both necessity and desire) remain highly personal, tactile and touchy-feely tokens in our lives. If you don't believe me, ask yourself how totally reluctant you are to ever hand your phone to someone else. You'll show them stuff on it all day, but sharing it with someone else is another story.

Right now, we're in the age of IG (Instant Gratification) and the immutable law of IWWIWWIWI. (I Want What I Want When I Want It). Every industry (even relatively new and fairly digital ones) will be changed significantly as we continue to move from the analog world to a world of digital everything. And new major businesses will be built in the cracks and the gaps created every time the big guys fall asleep at the switch.

Take gift cards, for example, and consider the very rapid rise of *Raise* (www.raise. com) which runs an online, mobile-enabled, exchange that sells partially used gift cards to consumers at a discount. And they don't <u>just</u> sell you the cards while you're sitting on the couch at home; they sell you the exact gift card that you need at a discount <u>while you're standing in the checkout line at the store</u>. Exactly what you need; precisely when you need it; and instantly. They sell you a *Target* gift card at a discount to the face amount of the card while you are standing in line getting ready to pay for your purchases at *Target*. Can you stand it? Can you even believe it? Well it's true. Right in the store. Right on the spot. And there's much, much more to come.

Your job is to anticipate how these kinds of game-changing shifts will impact your business because your business may be next in line. There are no simple answers, but there are a few things to watch for and to try to get in front of instead of waiting until it's too late and then spending a lot of costly and painful time playing catch-up.

(1) You need to constantly monitor and dynamically adjust the dollar allocations of your commitments to each of the channels you are using to reach your customers in as close to real time as possible. And the more channels you effectively employ, the higher your likelihood of ultimate success – especially because the vast majority of digital distribution channels are relatively ridiculously inexpensive to use.

(2) You need to monitor the ongoing migration of the traditional products and services in your sector or industry as they move from the analog and physical world into the new digital economy. Some will survive the transition; some will morph into new offerings; and some will cease to exist, but managing the life cycles of all of them will be crucial to your success.

(3) You need to watch for the emergence of new delivery channels and systems for both your own products and services and, more importantly, for the sale and delivery of competitive or substitute goods which may be better priced,

more readily accessible, easier to use; or more easily incorporated into the ways in which your customers are now conducting their own businesses.

(4) You need to watch for new consumer behaviors which are probably the most difficult to anticipate and also the most rapidly disruptive because of the speed and ease with which massive numbers of consumers can migrate to new solutions with virtually no switching costs or training requirements.

The bottom line never really changes. The customer has a constantly increasing array of choices, a limited attention span, and a relatively fixed amount to spend on whatever you're selling. The winners in the competition for those dollars will be the players who are most attentive to the customer's changing desires and most immediately responsive to their demands.

In the end, notwithstanding the appeal and power of the long tail, it's not a game of vast volume, it's always about the ultimate connection you build to your customers and the concrete value which you deliver for them.

IT'S ALL ABOUT HOLES, NOT DRILLS

One of the oldest clichés in business school is the statement that "customers want ¼" holes, not ¼"drills" which is a pithy way of simply reinforcing the idea that the primary focus and messaging in terms of presenting your product or service to the customer (and ultimately properly setting and then meeting his or her expectations) should be as closely aligned as possible with the results (benefits) that the customers are seeking rather than on other less critical features or concerns. People don't want copiers; they want clean, quick and inexpensive copies from machines that never break, jam or run out of toner.

Professor Clay Christensen describes this type of exercise and investigation as one where you are trying to correctly identify what the customer wants the product or service to do. In his classic example concerning breakfast beverages at McDonald's, he says the task is to figure out the job that the customer is "hiring" the milkshake to do. It turns out that that job was largely related to keeping early morning customers who were facing long commutes to the office from being bored as they drove. The milkshakes gave them something to do for an extended period of time and something to suck on while they whiled away the miles. So don't ever say that McShakes don't suck.

In earlier times, this results-oriented approach was known as "solution selling", but for me that particular phrase has taken on an interesting new meaning which grows out of a pretty fundamental change in the nature of many of the products we are now manufacturing.

In today's economy (except for consumables like toner and ink for our printers), the in-service life of all kinds of products has been so dramatically extended that the basic underlying business models of major manufacturers and entire industries have been changed. These days, (because the useful life of products which manufacturers could previously and reliably predict would become obsolete or used up in a reasonable timeframe) has now been lengthened to the point where they effectively last forever, the manufacturers have had to begin to re-envision their businesses.

No one smart thinks that they can simply sell a single product anymore. If you want to survive, you sell services and solutions – lifetime relationships and continuing connections - rather than transactional and occasional encounters. I wrote recently that the book business these days isn't about books anymore. (See http://www.inc. com/howard-tullman/the-case-for-pursuing-massive-growth.html) The point there was that the former publishers were all morphing their businesses into learning management companies which could sell protectable systems and services rather than individual books. The need for similar migratory movement is even clearer in various manufacturing sectors.

Take light bulbs for example. They don't burn out the way they used to and – as a result – the bulb manufacturers have basically improved themselves out of a major portion of what used to be their most consistent flow of recurring revenues. In any given cycle, they're selling fewer and fewer bulbs and there's zero prospect of a return to the old days. Even more importantly, after you've solved the power consumption issues and the longevity concerns; what do you really have left to sell to your customers or to differentiate your bulbs or fixtures from anyone else's?

The answer is that – and this is exactly what the big bulb guys are doing with their biggest institutional customers - you sell bundled "lighting" which is really the turn-key, all-in, "solution" that the customers are looking for rather than bulbs, fixtures, lumens, etc. and thus you avoid getting your brains beaten in and your margins crushed by price-based, foreign competitors. Lighting customers (big and little) just want to see where they're going and not worry about anything more than that. This approach is actually a return to the old days when the electric companies used to basically give you a bunch of bulbs for free from time to time as long as you'd come get them. Even back then, they knew that they were selling a solution and a service rather than a bunch of bulbs. And this is just the beginning.

Once you start thinking about the solution for a given problem like transportation – how, for example, do I most efficiently get from here to there - you start to focus on a broad range of available choices for intermodal transportation (planes, trains, buses and Ubers) rather than on the need to rent or own a particular form of vehicle. It's the same story with hotels and Airbnb – you're looking for clean, safe, inexpensive shelter – not a particular chain or brand of hotel. Utility, mobility, convenience and speed are all far more important to consumers today than possession or ownership and there's really no going back. (See http://www.inc.com/howard-tullman/why-gen-y-doesnt-care-about-cars.html)

AN OUNCE OF INTUITION IS WORTH A POUND OF PERSUASION

There's nothing quite like the feeling you get when your intuition pays off and people behave exactly as you predicted (and hoped for or dreaded) or when things turn out precisely as you expected. You could also call these moments the result of educated guesses or extra-sensory perceptions, but however you describe the process, the exhilaration's exactly the same. It's always a rush to be right.

It's not just a game of "I told you so" (although you did), it's really the satisfaction of knowing in your heart that these kinds of outcomes aren't actually just happy accidents or good breaks – they're another example in the long line of things that happen because you worked hard to make them happen. You always want to be driving the train, not chasing the caboose.

And there's nothing that makes the selling process easier than getting a jump on the customer and getting out in front of the competition by doing a little precision guesswork. It's just human nature that we'd all much prefer to be pulled in the direction toward which we were already inclined rather than pushed into something which we're not really sure is right for us or our business. Pounds of persuasion will never make up for even a little insight into what's really important and what's driving the customers' decisions. That's why I often say that - while it's hard to push a rope, it's actually pretty simple to pull a string. Or, as The Lone Ranger used to say: it's so much easier to ride the horse in the direction he's headed.

I have come to believe in matters of both intuition and magic in the way that Penn & Teller do – they show you how the trick is being done and you still can't figure out what exactly is going on. And what you take away from the experience of watching them perform is not some mystical sense (we all still know these are tricks); instead you leave feeling that you've witnessed the highest level of professionals executing difficult tasks in a craft that takes hundreds of hours of preparation, patter and patience.

It turns out that intuition – which can make or break so many things in your business and in your life – isn't something that's given only to the few. It's a skill that anyone can develop and one that grows more powerful as you continue to use it. Everyone has the same chance to build their own crystal ball – you just have to do the work and spend the time. It's exactly like the old saying about luck – the harder you work; the luckier you get. But first you have to know what the tools and techniques are that you should use in order to turn yourself into an intuitive wizard.

Get a Calendar and Track Your Customers' Schedules

So much of the world of business happens on a schedule and yet way too many people are either ignorant of that fact or oblivious to exactly how important timing is to successful sales. If your customers' aren't ready to listen or you're pitching them at the wrong time or place, it just doesn't matter what you're saying or what you've got to sell. I'm not talking simply about Salesforce ticklers or remembering someone's birthday; I'm talking about becoming a stone- cold expert on each client's procurement process and internal timing and planning cycles so you know how to be there when the customer is ready to buy. Too many salesmen in my life have returned empty-handed to report that they just missed the boat, they got beat out by someone who was there at the right time, or they got misled or misinformed by the client about their purchase schedule. You learn in this world that, in a lot of selling situations, the client doesn't want to say "No" to your face and so they tell you it's too soon or too early in their cycles to buy or commit until finally one day when they break the bad news to you that they went elsewhere. Just remember that in sales "it's always too soon until it's too late". Do your homework.

Anticipate and Prepare for the "Second Sale"

There's really no telling what's going to happen in the room when the customer and his finance team get together to review and decide whether to renew your arrangements with them. This is the "second sale" and it's even more critical than the first. Sadly, you won't be there, but that doesn't mean you can't influence the outcome by making sure that you have an advocate in the room (word to the wise – it will never be the bean counters) and that you have provided your spokesperson with the support, the cost benefits, the time savings, and the other justifications – basically all the ammunition necessary – in order to support the idea of staying in business with you. This stuff doesn't happen by itself and the customer rarely takes the initiative to go to bat for you. It's on you to make sure that there's a compelling case and lots of reasons to renew and that you get it in front of the right people at the right time.

Listen to the Customer and Put Yourself in Their Shoes

Many of us think that our customers are really good at complaining and making their feelings known, but the truth is that they aren't. They don't want to spend their time telling us what isn't working for them (or why) and they certainly don't want to argue about whose fault that is. Anyone who tells you that the customer understands that a given problem is <u>their</u> fault is an idiot. There are <u>no</u> customer problems. By and large, unhappy customers don't typically spend a lot of time sharing and communicating because they don't think that's their job. They get nervous or unhappy and things build and develop from there, but they rarely go out of their way to let you know. When they reach their limits, they just pick up and leave. It's your job to read the tea leaves, ask the questions that no one else is asking and get them the answers before the building burns down. Sometimes no one wants to ask the critical questions because it means hard conversations, tough choices and more work for people who are already busy and otherwise occupied. But that's small potatoes compared to losing the business or the customer or the tenant.

The bottom line: renewals are just business; terminations are personal and surprises are the worst of all. But, if you do your job and pay attention to your business and your customers – meeting their current needs and expectations - and anticipating their future desires and requirements, they'll think for sure that you've got a crystal ball hidden somewhere.

IT'S MY PARTY AND
I'LL BUY IF I WANT TO

Customer segmentation has been around as an essential business practice for ages. In fact, the age (or range of ages) of various customers has always been one of the more obvious ways in which merchants and other service providers could slice and dice their potential consumer and business targets into theoretically distinguishable clusters whose needs and interests could be distinctly and differently identified and addressed in bulk. Gender, geography, graduation levels, etc. were other basic criteria which fed into generalized profiles and composites. Credit, race, political views and other less politically correct characterizations also made their way into the calculations as often as not.

But, as with everything else today, new and better personalization data and other measurement and location-sensitive identification tools are rapidly changing the game and the ground rules for sales success. It's not enough to know who I am and what I'm interested in although that's a decent starting point. Mass customization is the minimum goal and very little will be left to deal with in grossly simplistic terms or in bulk because every consumer today wants to believe that they're being treated as individuals and they want to make their purchasing decisions by the bite or the byte on a one-off basis. One size no longer fits almost anyone and the greatest sin of all is to take any of your customers or prospects for granted.

At the same time, what is still somewhat surprising in this all-digital, all-the-time, world is that - in addition to the new learnings which the data can now provide about almost every customer's desires and objectives which will further increase our ability to individualize our offerings and responses - many of the consequences, strategies and prescriptions growing out of the latest research are primarily physical in nature rather than digital.

Think of this as the latest version of "retail revisited" - not as a fad or even a trend, but as a major shift in the ways that traditional retail space will need to accommodate new customer concerns and requirements. See http://www.inc.com/howard-tullman/the-future-of-self-service.html . We'll be building new and different spaces containing smaller, more personal, environments which will best suit the new mobile and constantly-connected customers whom we expect to attract and also permit us to adapt on the fly to the desires of each and every entrant – new or returning – based on their needs at the time.

Comprehensive use of demographic data will be useful, but no longer a competitive differentiation. And even basic "interest" and social information (far more critical today than mere customer attributes) won't be sufficient to win the battle because the new behavior drivers won't be uniform or consistent even on an individual basis. Some expected, routine and consistent behaviors which are fairly reliable will be ascertainable, but the real winners will understand that - each time a customer now appears - it's essentially a brand-new day dictated and determined in the moment by the customer's then-dominant and most pressing desires.

Customers will continue to fall into new distinct categories, but the categories will vary over time in significant ways. My shorthand for these variable behaviors is to think of them as "objectives". What's the customer's goal and how can the environment and the staff best facilitate the success of the customer's quest to achieve it? See http://www.inc.com/howard-tullman/whats-wrong-with-retail-and-what-does-it-mean-for-you/html.html . In a sense, this is simply an effort to peel the consumer onion a little more and get tighter and tighter views of the customer, but at the moment, no one is even thinking about looking at the customer through this new lens.

And while some "goal" creep and overlapping or inconsistent desires are certain to occur for some customers, once you start organizing your approach and your thinking around this new perspective, you're going to find that it's fairly easy to understand and appreciate its importance, but very complicated to implement an in-store program to address it. It's simple to see because it's absolutely applicable to you and me as well as to everyone else, but it's hard to address all the different requirements of the various individuals.

Here are some of the competing profiles and customer expectations which the retail environments of tomorrow (which actually means right now) will need to accommodate. Now's the time to start thinking about how your business or service can address them.

1. Mission (In and Out) versus Discovery (Time to Explore & Learn)

Time is the scarcest resource of all today and mission-driven shoppers want to be in and out of the store as quickly as possible. We live in a world of instant gratification. The shoppers like express checkout lines manned by real people and they hate self-checkout systems which they know will take them twice as long to use for the few items they have purchased. ATMs are a whole lot faster and easier than tellers, but scanners are still slow and difficult. Explorers, on the other hand, are there with a different purpose – they're willing to commit the time it takes to find new and unusual offerings – to experiment with new choices and to learn about new alternatives. They're the pioneers of the entertainment economy where the experience is the most important aspect of the encounter. These are the ripest targets for in-store sampling, demo stations, special offers and even videos. They're in the food lane and not the fast lane and they're in no hurry. And it's a phenomena that's by no means limited to groceries. You know the times are changing when the quality of a new car's sound system and its Wi-Fi connectivity are as (or more) important to the purchasing decision as the car's performance.

2. Choice (Super Selection) versus Convenience (Front and Center – Grab and Go)

A significant amount of research over the years has gone into the paralyzing effect on choosers of too many choices – it often results in no action at all - and this problem sets up another challenge for retailers. Overwhelming the consumer with massive displays and innumerable choices and emphasizing selection works for some folks, but it can be very off-putting to the customer who knows just what he or she wants and is brand-loyal as well. We're going to see mini-stores within the bigger boxes, but not ones dedicated to marketers like Microsoft or Samsung or P&G. The minis coming soon to stores near you will be choice-constrained and filled with the most frequently and consistently purchased items so I can grab what I need and get out. Using the back walls of the big box for dairy products in order to pull the shopper through the stores is a strategy that just won't work any longer for a significant segment of the audience. In fact, more and more customers will be ordering bulk items and commodities that they would typically buy every week online by subscription or fulfillment services and not trying to drag the same stuff home from the market every week.

3. Click and Pick (Drive-Thru) versus Park and Party (Time to Kill)

Same day delivery is coming soon (one hour delivery for Amazon Prime customers is already rolling out in major markets), but it still may not be fast enough to beat what's exploding all over Europe – click (buy online) and pick (drive to the store to get it) has become amazingly popular – especially with Moms – who'd rather throw the kids in the car and make three quick pickups (without ever even parking) at her favorite stores instead of sitting at home and hoping for the delivery guy to show. More than 30% of several major retailers' holiday sales last season were in-store pickups of goods ordered online and the trend continues to accelerate. But again, that approach only serves some of the shoppers. A different group of people goes to the store because they have nothing else to do. They're anxious to lose themselves in the store for as long as possible because they've got time to kill and nowhere else important to be. They'll be quick to grab a bite at in-store food service operations – not because they're famished - but because they're anxious to get off their feet. Having the snack shops at the front of the store – beyond the registers and post-checkout – is another design idea whose time has come and gone.

There are plenty of additional examples and there's not a business around that won't do far better if it adapts its facilities to accommodate all these variable demands and - at the same time - adapts its sales approach to each customer's specific goals. It's not that hard to quickly figure out what's driving each customer, but if you aren't focused on finding this out, your customers will quickly find someplace else that has and do their shopping there.

NOT EVERY NICHE
LEADS TO NIRVANA

I try to be open and receptive to every new idea for a product or service that's presented to me because it's part of my job to be a good listener and to evaluate new business ideas and because you can learn something valuable from almost every pitch – sometimes it's exactly what you should also be thinking about (and maybe already doing) in the context of your own business – and sometimes it's something that you wouldn't consider doing in a month of Sundays. I learned long ago that you can have the very best of intentions and still have a really bad idea.

But, in any case, it's generally a good investment of the modest amount of time it takes to pay attention and be polite unless the people pitching haven't done their homework, don't appreciate or want to hear about the magnitude or difficulty of what they're setting out to do, or just aren't really prepared to effectively present and defend their ideas. No one these days has time to waste listening to half-baked businesses or fever dreams. Everyone's entitled to their own ideas (good or bad), but not to their own reality. And another hard-learned lesson is that there is virtually no consistent correlation between great talkers and great ideas. Ideas are driven by enthusiasm, but success depends on execution – you can't win a race with your mouth.

And lately, I feel like we're having another unfortunate run of what I call "slice it and dice it" disease. The premise of all these pitches is that you can take any good idea for a product, service or network (typically someone else's idea who is already hitting it out of the park) and shrink that business down to a narrower target population or a specific niche or a certain kind of consumer and instantly turn the process of serving that smaller segment into a big business as well. Messaging apps just for Moms. Social networks strictly for softball players. Reward programs restricted to redheads. You name it.

I do often say these days that - because of the Internet - niches are no longer necessarily small, but that doesn't mean that they're any easier to address and conquer or that – in fact – while the barriers to entry are deceptively low, the barriers to success aren't even higher than ever. You still need a compelling reason for people to use your product or service and to change their behaviors to do so. Even relatively new habits are hard to break. And while it's true that one size never fits all, it doesn't follow that there's an infinite demand for things in every possible size, shape or variety. Different isn't always better.

And frankly as pervasive as the idea is that we can monetize everything that any of us has in excess (I call this "the emerging surplus economy"), I don't see the whole world being Uber-ized any time soon. We'll see hundreds of variations on this theme, but very few valuable businesses will survive after the novelty wears off and the difficulties of delivering these types of programs at scale becomes increasingly apparent. Uber everything is pretty much a pipe dream.

But if you insist on slicing the salami and heading down this long and winding road and if you're intent on building the next luxury linen outlet just for little people or something even more exotic and esoteric, ask yourself these three questions first:

(1) <u>Who Really Needs Another Whatever?</u>

We've all got more stuff than we need. More friends and followers than we could ever keep up with. More apps and programs on our devices than we can even remember. And more devices than we know what to do with. And you want to add your pony to the pile? I don't think so. I'm afraid that most of the boats have sailed, most of the folks have decided what they're interested in, where they spend their time, and what they pay attention to, and it's gonna be really hard to explain to them why they need another anything.

And your offering isn't even another anything exactly – it's sort of a particular piece of what they already have a bunch of in several variations. It's like offering someone a new email address. Most people would rather poke their eyes out than have to start checking another mailbox and that's even assuming that you could convince them that the effort was worth the time. What exactly are you offering that isn't redundant and duplicative – even if it's slightly more targeted and focused? Most folks have figured out the basic filters that help cut down on the crap they're seeing every day and all the big guys are already adding built-in (and often default) ad blockers to try to delay the inevitable and ongoing migration from websites and email to messaging services which is accelerating every day among the mobile millions and putting a critical damper on online web ad sales. It's really hard to see how you'll even get your message out there to these targets who are doing everything in their power to shut down the volume and turn off the spigot. The most likely outcome is that you'll be left in the dust at the starting gate or trampled by the crowd because you don't have a clear and concise answer to why anyone needs what you're selling.

(2) Who Could Do the Same Thing in a New York Minute?

If it's a remotely good idea, there are hundreds of businesses much bigger and more established than you with millions of existing users who are exactly the people/prospects you want to pitch. All of these competitors (and potentially very fast followers) are searching every day for more products, services and solutions to offer their users since they are under tremendous pressure to constantly engage and retain them. They have no new acquisition costs. They have already built the necessary pipeline and technology. And they are just waiting to steal your idea if it's any good and serve it up to their customers. Nothing you have is gonna stop them, but if you stay small enough, maybe they won't notice you. And the thought that they will swoop in and buy your baby business instead of ripping you off and building their own is another bad bet which happens roughly once in a blue moon.

(3) Who Will Pay Anything for It?

Your friends and family may think your idea is terrific and you might easily recruit a talented team to take on the challenge with you since everyone wants to be an entrepreneur today, but remember that there's an infinite demand for the unavailable and you won't know a thing for certain until you have something to sell that lots of people want to buy, be part of, or otherwise support. Nothing happens without customers and sales. We buy things because we think they are worth more to us than we are paying for them and – more importantly – when we are convinced that they deliver something we don't now have, but definitely want. Businesses need to be built first on revenues from real people and then they can expand their model to incorporate advertising and other income streams. But the dream of building a large population first (and basically for nothing) so it can be marketed and sold to advertisers who will pay to access these folks is simply a nightmare today. It's an old story (and an even older movie) – it's not clear that it ever worked over the long haul for anyone (Twitter seems to still be looking for an answer while their user base continues to plummet) - and I can assure you that you will also run out of money and starve long before your attempt to crack the code goes anywhere.

Nirvana is that moment of insight and stillness of mind – of perfect clarity - when all the passions, all the delusions and all the frenzy have been driven away. When you have to look in the mirror and face the facts. And when you do you'll see that not every niche leads to nirvana.

ABOUT THE AUTHOR

Howard Tullman is the CEO of 1871 in Chicago where digital startups get their start. He is also the General Managing Partner of two venture funds: Chicago High- Tech Investment Partners and G2T3V, LLC, which both focus on funding disruptive innovators. He is the former Chairman and CEO of Tribeca Flashpoint Media Arts Academy in Chicago. He is an active member of numerous city, state and civic boards and organizations and a tireless supporter and mentor to many start-ups and other businesses and individuals. He has successfully founded more than a dozen high-tech businesses in his 50 year career and created more than $1 billion in investor value as well as thousands of new jobs. He writes a regular weekly blog on The Perspiration Principles for Inc. Magazine and can be directly contacted:

- by email at h@1871.com
- on twitter @tullman
- his blog: tullman.blogspot.com
- his primary website: www.tullman.com

To get all of Howard's blog posts in one download, visit Blogintobook.com/tullman/.